General Editors: Professor A.N. Jeffares (*University of Stirling*) & Professor Suheil Bushrui (*American University of Beirut*)

George Bernard Shaw

SAINT JOAN

Notes by Anne Wright

BA PH D (LONDON)
Head of English Literature, Hatfield Polytechnic

LONGMAN
YORK PRESS

YORK PRESS
Immeuble Esseily, Place Riad Solh, Beirut.

LONGMAN GROUP LIMITED
Longman House,
Burnt Mill,
Harlow,
Essex

© Librairie du Liban 1984

First published 1984
ISBN 0 582 78286 4
Printed in Hong Kong by
Wilture Printing Co Ltd.

Contents

Part 1

Introduction

SHAW IS UNDOUBTEDLY one of the greatest dramatists to have written in English, second perhaps only to Shakespeare. His plays have been translated into many languages, and are performed and read all over the world. His prolific output as a playwright spanned more than half a century, from 1892 to 1949; indeed, in many ways Shaw's writing expresses the transition from the Victorian age to the modern world.

Early life in Ireland

George Bernard Shaw chose to live most of his adult life in England. However, by birth and nationality he was Irish, born in Dublin on 26 July 1856. In 1876 he left Ireland to come to London, where he made his home for many years. Voluntary exile may have sharpened Shaw's awareness of national attitudes, and contributed to the ironic detachment with which he was able to view and write about the problems of society. Also, his childhood in Dublin alerted him to class and religious differences. His family was Irish Protestant, in a mainly Roman Catholic community. Bernard was brought up as a Protestant, and attended church and Sunday School, although he soon rejected Christianity. Later in life Shaw claimed that the short period he spent in a school where most of the pupils were Catholics made him feel acutely ashamed and out of place. This feeling was one of social as well as religious awkwardness. Irish Protestantism aligned itself with the wealthy governing class, as well as with England and with the northern province of Ulster. Shaw belonged to what he called the 'shabby genteel' class, with social aspirations beyond its financial means. His father, George Carr Shaw, ran a wholesale corn business which was not very successful. However he, and even more Mrs Shaw, liked to emphasise the family's associations with the gentry, and they regarded themselves as socially superior to those around them, even to people more affluent than they were.

The family life of the Shaw household was not wholly conventional. George Carr Shaw was a secret drinker, a fact which lessened Bernard's respect for him and influenced his own lifelong abstinence from alcohol. However, it seems that his father also had a positive influence on Shaw; George had a strong sense of humour, and his son came to share his irreverence for established institutions, and his scorn for sentimentality and romance. Shaw's mother was of a reserved disposition, not given to displays of emotion or affection. Dissatisfied with her marriage to an unsuccessful and alcoholic husband, she devoted her considerable energies and ability to music. From his mother Shaw gained an early acquaintance with music, and in particular a love of opera which persisted throughout his life. Mrs Shaw was an independent and determined woman, as well as a talented singer. She pursued her musical career in Dublin with the help of her singing teacher, George John Vandaleur Lee. This rather eccentric man lived with the Shaw family for a number of years, before leaving for London. In 1872 Mrs Shaw followed him with her two daughters, one of whom, Lucy Carr Shaw, was also to take up singing as a career (the other, Agnes, died a few years later). Meanwhile, Bernard Shaw had left school in 1871, when he was fifteen. He had not distinguished himself as a scholar, and had no wish to continue formal education by proceeding to university. All his life, Shaw stressed his self-education by reading and experience, in ideas, music and drama. On leaving school he worked for a firm of land agents in Dublin, first as a clerk and then as a cashier. In 1876 he left this employment and joined his mother in London, where he obtained a job with a telephone company.

London 1876–1892

During his early years in London Shaw continued the process of self-education, reading widely and attending public lectures on a variety of topics. He was influenced in his decision to become a vegetarian, in 1881, partly by reading Shelley and partly by a friend, Henry Salt. At this time Shaw made a number of influential friends, including Sidney (1859–1947) and Beatrice (1858–1943) Webb, William Morris (1834–96) and Karl Marx's daughter Eleanor (1855–98). These friendships developed alongside his interests, artistic, intellectual and political. In the 1880s debating societies were extremely popular in London, and Shaw joined several of these, developing an ability to speak in public. He also wrote five novels. None was accepted by a publisher, although all except the first were serialised in magazines.

Shaw had more success in becoming a journalist than as a novelist. He obtained his first appointment, as art critic to *The World*, in 1886, through his friend, the journalist, drama critic and translator William Archer. From the mid 1880s Shaw was able to make a living by writing for newspapers and journals. He wrote book reviews for the *Pall Mall Gazette* (1885), and music criticism for *The Star* (1888–94). He was a particularly talented music critic, writing his entertaining and well-informed pieces on concerts and opera in London under the pseudonym of 'Corno di Bassetto'. Later Shaw became drama critic for *The Saturday Review* (1895–8). His collected criticism, published in three volumes under the title *Our Theatres in the Nineties*, is a valuable record of the theatre in London at that time.

Politics

In 1882 Shaw attended a lecture given by Henry George, the American author of *Progress and Poverty*, and was converted to socialism. He also read one volume of Marx's *Das Kapital* (in a French translation, as no English version was then available). He was active in the Marxist Social Democratic Federation, where he came into contact with William Morris and Eleanor Marx, and subsequently, in 1884, he joined the newly formed Fabian Society. Shaw and the Webbs, Sidney and Beatrice, became leading figures in the Fabian Society, shaping its commitment to working towards socialism by constitutional means. The Fabians were mainly middle-class intellectuals. Sidney and Beatrice Webb were dedicated sociologists, whose ideas and influence were later felt in the developing Labour movement. With Shaw they founded the London School of Economics, and the journal *The New Statesman*. The Fabians recognised Shaw's ability to publicise and promote their socialist ideas. He wrote many pamphlets for the Fabian Society, and edited and contributed to the *Fabian Essays in Socialism* (1889). His later political writings, such as *The Intelligent Woman's Guide to Socialism and Capitalism* (1928) and *Everybody's Political What's What* (1944) still maintain the Fabian stance of rejection of revolution and militancy in favour of gradual, parliamentary reform, stressing the importance of education. Shaw was not however opposed in principle to direct action (and indeed he took part in the riots which came to be known as Bloody Sunday in Trafalgar Square in 1887); he considered that a revolution was unlikely to establish socialism in England, and that in any case it was more practical and wiser in the long term to make use of the experience of the existing machinery of government.

Ibsenism

The plays of Henrik Ibsen (1828–1906) dealt in a realistic manner with the problems of contemporary society. Ibsen challenged the institutions of marriage and the family, and questioned the value placed by conventional morality on virtues such as conformity, piety and respectability. Early performances of his plays met with extreme hostility. Audiences were shocked by their references to topics then considered unmentionable in polite society, such as venereal disease and incest (in

Ghosts). *A Doll's House* was performed in England in 1889, and *Ghosts* in 1891. In the early 1890s fashionable society was divided between hailing Ibsen as a great dramatist and novelist, and rejecting his work as immoral and obscene; and Ibsenism became associated with progressive minorities such as the campaigners for women's rights.

Shaw gave a favourable review to the production of *A Doll's House*, and defended the play in the *Pall Mall Gazette*. In 1890 he delivered a lecture on Ibsen as one of a series on 'Socialism in Contemporary Literature' arranged by the Fabian Society. The lecture was subsequently expanded and published as *The Quintessence of Ibsenism* in 1891. In this treatise, which was the first in English to be written on Ibsen, Shaw describes him as dramatising the conflict between realism and false sentimentality, and between conservatism and the pressure for social change. Social evolution takes place through the replacement of outmoded values and ideals by new ones; but the individuals who argue for such change are typically seen as immoral. Ibsen's characters are divided into realists who display common sense and progressive attitudes, and idealists who cling to outmoded institutions. His portrayal of female figures recognises that the stereotype of feminine domesticity must be rejected if women are to become emancipated. Shaw's account of Ibsen is influenced by the purpose of the lecture from which it developed, and, to an extent, by his own interests and point of view. The ideas on social evolution, and the role of women in society, may be related to Shaw's ideas on the Life Force and Creative Evolution. His own play-writing was also influenced by Ibsen, particularly in the early stages of his career. Shaw revised *The Quintessence of Ibsenism* in 1912–13, adding sections on the plays which had been written after the first edition was published.

Creative Evolution

Shaw lost his faith in Protestant Christianity while he was still in Dublin. However, although he remained an atheist for the rest of his life, Shaw was in the broad sense religious, and he formulated a personal philosophy of creative evolution based on secular theories. Charles Darwin's (1809–82) *On the Origin of Species* (1859) was a pervasive intellectual influence in the latter part of the nineteenth century. Shaw saw the implications of Darwin's biological theory of evolution for religion, morality, and psychology. He rejected the determinism of natural selection, because it endorsed ruthless competition in society, and because philosophically it denied the possibility of conscious willed intervention in the process of evolution. Instead Shaw followed Samuel Butler, author of *The Way of All Flesh* (1903), in postulating a will beyond the individual, striving for the improvement of the species.

This notion of the non-individual will has much in common with the philosophies of Friedrich Nietzsche (1844–1900) and Artur Schopenhauer (1788–1860). Shaw also found support for the doctrine of creative evolution in the writings of the French philosopher Henri Bergson (1859–1941), whose *élan vital* is the equivalent of Shaw's Life Force or Evolutionary Appetite.

The ideas of creative evolution contribute to Shaw's plays. In *Man and Superman* (1903), the heroine Ann Whitefield is the instrument of the Life Force; her marriage to Jack Tanner fulfils the impersonal biological urge of the woman to reproduce and improve the species. Women in Shaw's plays often possess intuitive gifts which he associates with the Life Force: Mrs George in *Getting Married* has visionary trances; *Major Barbara* is inspired by her faith; and Joan's voices are an expression of her evolutionary appetite. *Back to Methuselah* shows the emergence in the far distant future of a race of superior beings with visionary powers. This cycle of plays and its Preface (1921) are Shaw's fullest statement of the ideas of creative evolution.

Christianity

Shaw made use in his writing of the Christian concepts and terminology familiar to him from his Protestant upbringing. Although he was a materialist, with no faith in the supernatural or in a life after death, he adapted the concepts of salvation and damnation, heaven and hell to express his own secular religion. Socialism, for example, is described in his writing as a kind of collective salvation, which is the equivalent of the kingdom of heaven on earth. Christian characters and institutions figure in a number of Shaw's plays. Salvation is a central theme of *Major Barbara* (1905), whose heroine is a convert to the Salvation Army. *Androcles and the Lion* (1912) presents a group of early Christian martyrs in imperial Rome. In *Saint Joan* (1924) Joan comes into conflict with the authority of the medieval Church. In the Preface to *Androcles and the Lion* Shaw explains his objections to Christian doctrines of redemption and atonement, and analyses the Gospels. The tale of *The Adventures of the Black Girl in her Search for God* (1932) compares various religions and concepts of God. It employs the ideas of creative evolution in its conclusion that God is not perfect or finished, but a goal towards which mankind is continuously striving. Although Shaw did not profess a formal religion, his writing expresses a coherent and consistent morality based on a system of values. Central to this morality is the notion, also fundamental to Christianity, of the responsibility of the individual to himself, to society and to the species.

1892–1898: Early career as a dramatist

His work as a drama critic for *The Saturday Review* exposed Shaw to the current fashions of the London theatre. He had however been a keen theatre-goer since his boyhood in Dublin. In the nineteenth century the theatre was regarded primarily as a medium for entertainment, using a variety of forms including melodrama, pantomime, burlesque (a satirical comedy, usually with music), opera, dramatic comedy and farce, as well as tragedy and spectacular historical romance. Productions of Shakespeare made drastic alterations to the text and concentrated on enhancing the central role of the star performer. Theatrical companies were formed by actor-managers such as Henry Irving, who received great adulation and was honoured with a knighthood. The London theatre of the 1890s catered for audiences drawn from fashionable society. One of the most favoured and popular forms was the 'well-made play', which was a polished but essentially contrived and mechanical elaboration of a simple dramatic situation. Shaw denounced such plays as superficial and sensational. When he came to write plays himself, he drew on the available dramatic forms, but exploited and modified them in such a way as to reveal their empty conventionality, and develop his own serious themes.

Shaw's first play, *Widowers' Houses*, was completed in 1892 for performance by the Independent Theatre as a successor to Ibsen's *Ghosts*. This play and *Mrs Warren's Profession* (1893) focused on specific social problems, slum housing and prostitution, such as were the subject of Shaw's tracts and pamphlets for the Fabian Society. They were not a theatrical success, and indeed *Mrs Warren's Profession* was banned from public performance by the censor, the Lord Chamberlain. Shaw went on to write romantic comedy, in such plays as *Arms and the Man* (1894) and *Candida* (1897). *The Devil's Disciple* (1897) used the convention of melodrama and in *The Man of Destiny* (1895) and *Caesar and Cleopatra* (1899) he tried his hand at historical drama. Shaw published his early work as *Plays Unpleasant and Pleasant* (1898), and *Three Plays for Puritans* (1901).

In 1898, Shaw married Charlotte Payne-Townshend, a wealthy heiress with socialist convictions. Theirs was a celibate marriage, and they remained close companions until Charlotte's death in 1943. After living for several years in London they moved to the village of Ayot St Lawrence in Hertfordshire. Shaw conducted flirtations with several famous actresses, largely by correspondence. He had flirted with Ellen Terry before he was married; the most notorious such relationship after his marriage was with Mrs Patrick Campbell, who played Eliza in *Pygmalion*.

1900–1914: Success as a dramatist

Between 1900 and the outbreak of the First World War Shaw wrote a number of major plays, which brought him commercial success and established his reputation as a dramatist. The plays written during this period include *Man and Superman* (1903), *Major Barbara* (1905), *The Doctor's Dilemma* (1908) and *Pygmalion* (1912). From 1904 to 1907 Shaw's new plays received their first production at the Court Theatre in the seasons of repertory put on by Harley Granville Barker and T. E. Vedrenne, alongside Greek classics, and the work of modern European dramatists and the newer English playwrights. Barker was dedicated to the recognition of drama as a serious artistic form, and he and Shaw campaigned for the establishment of a National Theatre. *In Getting Married* (1908) and *Misalliance* (1910) Shaw moved further away from action-filled plots, towards plays based entirely on discussion of ideas.

The First World War

Shaw was too old to fight in the First World War, but he was deeply affected by it. His long article 'Common Sense about the War', which was printed as a supplement to the *New Statesman* in 1914, caused an uproar. Shaw maintained that England and Germany were equally to blame for what happened, and criticised the incompetence and ignorance of politicians and military leaders. He deplored excessive patriotism and misplaced heroism, which sentimentalised and romanticised war. As the conflict dragged on, however, Shaw came to consider that the immediate national crisis must take temporary priority over the cause of international socialism, and hoped therefore that England would defeat Germany. In 1917 he was invited, as a prominent public figure, to make an official visit to the Western Front in Flanders.

During the war Shaw wrote several topical playlets on issues such as recruiting, and the civilian war effort, some of which were performed to audiences of soldiers. One of his greatest plays, *Heartbreak House*, was written in 1916–17. It depicts society as being on the point of destruction, although it refers only indirectly and symbolically to the actual war. In the Preface (1919) Shaw explained that *Heartbreak House* could not be produced during the war, when the theatre became once again a place for light entertainment rather than serious drama. By the time this play was produced in England in 1921, Shaw had also written his 'Biological Pentateuch', *Back to Methuselah*. After the war Shaw was optimistic that the international effort of President Wilson and the League of Nations would guarantee permanent peace, but his hopes of a political solution to the problems of society gradually waned.

Saint Joan

Shaw regained his popularity in the theatre with *Saint Joan*. The subject was topical, as Joan had recently been canonised. However, as early as 1913, Shaw had written to Mrs Patrick Campbell when he was on holiday in Orléans, that he would one day write a play about Joan of Arc. In 1923 a friend gave Shaw a copy of an account of the trial of Joan written by T. Douglas Murray and entitled *Jeanne d'Arc, Maid of Orleans, Deliverer of France* (1902). Charlotte Shaw read it first, and suggested to her husband that Joan would be a suitable subject for his next play. Shaw began writing *Saint Joan* on 29 April 1923; the play was finished by the end of August. It was first published in a German translation, as *Die heilige Johanna*, in the *Neue Rundschau* (Berlin), June-September 1924. The first English edition appeared in the same year. *Saint Joan* was first performed by the Theatre Guild at the Garrick Theatre, New York, on 28 December 1923. The British première took place at the New Theatre, London, on 26 March 1924, with Sybil Thorndike as Joan. The production was a commercial success, and the play was favourably received by both Catholics and Protestants. It has been performed many times since then, and the role of Joan rapidly became a favourite with actresses.

Shaw was keen that *Saint Joan* should be filmed, and in 1934 he adapted the play for the screen. His screenplay made cuts here and there and added scenes, with or without extra dialogue. However, the project encountered financial difficulties, as Shaw could not reach agreement with his sponsors over arrangements for his own income from the film. Moreover, the Italian group Catholic Action condemned Shaw's play because its historical interpretation did not concur with the official view of the Catholic Church. It also appeared likely that the newly agreed code of film censorship in the United States would ban distribution of the film. The result was that the project to film *Saint Joan* was abandoned. Ingrid Bergman, whom Shaw had nominated for the part of Joan, appeared instead in a film, *Joan of Arc*, based on a play by Maxwell Anderson. Shaw's *Saint Joan* was filmed in 1957 by the director Otto Preminger. The screenplay was by the Catholic novelist Graham Greene, who altered the play to conform with the official Church view of Joan's trial.

1924–1950

In his later years Shaw was a famous and respected dramatist and man of letters. In 1925 he was awarded the Nobel Prize for literature. In 1929 the Malvern Festival was founded by Sir Barry Jackson for the performance of Shaw's plays and the music of Edward Elgar. Shaw's later plays include several with a political subject: *The Apple Cart*

(1929), *On the Rocks* (1933) and *Geneva* (1938). In *Too True to be Good* (1932) and *The Simpleton of the Unexpected Isles* (1935) he experimented with the non-realistic 'extravaganza'. *In Good King Charles's Golden Days* (1939) is another historical drama, in the form of a discussion.

In 1931 Shaw was invited to visit Moscow, where he met Stalin. His praise for Soviet achievements, and his later defence of Stalin, Mussolini and Hitler, as examples of strong leadership, earned him disfavour. However, these political attitudes were a development of his earlier socialist convictions. After Charlotte Shaw's death in 1943, Shaw continued to write plays, at his home in Ayot St Lawrence. He died on 4 November 1950, at the age of ninety-four.

Historical background of *Saint Joan*

The Hundred Years' War (1338–1453)

This is the name given to the long period of conflict between England and France, although the two countries were actually at war for only a small fraction of the time. Causes of the war included economic and commercial rivalry, focusing on the wool trade of Flanders and wine trade of Gascony. Political considerations involved England's claim to large areas of French territory, and the disputed sovereignty of France.

In 1337 Edward III of England had put forward a claim to the French throne. In 1346 he landed on the coast of Normandy, defeated the French forces at Crécy, and captured Calais. In 1356 Edward's son, the Black Prince, defeated the French at Poitiers and captured John II, king of France. A truce followed in 1360, with another spate of fighting after 1369 and a further truce in 1396. Henry V revived the English claim to the French throne and invaded France, gaining a victory at Agincourt in 1415. By the treaty of Troyes (1420) the French throne reverted from Charles VI to Henry V's heir, and Charles's son the Dauphin, later Charles VII, was repudiated as illegitimate. In 1422, however, both Henry V and Charles VI died. Henry VI was a minor, and his cause was hindered by the breakdown of the Anglo-Burgundian alliance. When Joan of Arc appeared on the scene in 1428, the crown was still the subject of a dispute between the Dauphin Charles and the English King Henry VI. Henry's armies, in alliance with the Burgundians, occupied northern France. The Dauphin was still uncrowned six years after his father's death, and Rheims, the place of consecration, was within the territory held by his enemies.

When the English began the siege of Orléans in 1428, Joan of Arc's intervention assisted the French to deliver the town, and marked a turning point in the war. Charles's coronation took place on July 17, 1429, in Rheims Cathedral, with Joan present. In 1435 Charles made a separate peace with Burgundy and captured Paris. A period of military inactivity followed. Between 1449 and 1461, when Charles died, the English were driven out of France. In 1453 Bordeaux was re-occupied by the French, and only Calais remained in English hands.

Joan of Arc

Joan was born *c*. 1412 at Domrémy, between Champagne and Lorraine. At the age of thirteen she began to hear voices from God, and to see visions of St Michael, St Catherine, and St Margaret, the patron saints of her country. Led by her voices she travelled in May 1428, and again in January 1429, to Vaucouleurs, where she obtained the local captain's permission to join the Dauphin at Chinon. The Dauphin provided her with troops: she marched to Orléans, entered the city on 29 April 1429, and in a series of engagements between 6 May and 8 May delivered it from siege. Her forces were subsequently victorious at Beaugency and Patay. On 16 July Rheims opened its gates to Charles, and his coronation took place the following day. Compiègne, Beauvais, Senlis and other towns north of Paris surrendered to the King, and on 28 August a four months' truce was signed with the Burgundians. Encouraged by the resistance of Paris, the Burgundians made a recovery. In the spring of 1430, the Duke of Burgundy attacked Compiègne.

In May 1430 Joan was captured while leading a sortie from Compiègne. John of Luxembourg and the Duke of Burgundy handed her over to the Bishop of Beauvais, in the name of the English king, upon payment of ten thousand francs. The trial was held in Rouen. Joan was interrogated a number of times between 21 February and 24 March, and the trial proper began a few days later. On 23 May she was informed that if she persisted in her errors she would be handed over to the secular authorities for punishment. She signed a form of abjuration on 24 May, but a few days later was held to have relapsed. She was burnt at the stake on 30 May 1431.

In 1450, Charles VII ordered an enquiry into the trial in order to clear his royal title. In 1456, proceedings inaugurated by Pope Calixtus III revoked and annulled the sentence of 1431. Joan was canonised by Pope Benedict XV on 16 May 1920, and her feast is celebrated on 30 May. On 24 June 1920, the French parliament decreed a national festival in her honour, to be held on the second Sunday in May.

The feudal system

The term feudalism denotes a social system of rights and duties based on land tenure, and on specified personal relationships. A number of societies have passed through a feudal period in their history. The European feudal system originated in the eighth century, when the Franks entered Gaul following the collapse of the Roman Empire; it subsequently underwent internal development during the ninth century. Land was held by vassals or feudal lords in 'fief' from their overlord or king, to whom they paid allegiance, including the duty to provide military support. Social cohesion derived from this relationship of vassal and overlord; the system was accordingly essentially individual and local rather than national.

The manor or estate held by the feudal lord was a social, economic and administrative unit devoted to agricultural production. The peasants – 'serfs' or 'villeins' – received from their manorial lord strips of land for cultivation and rights of pasturage, in return for dues in the form of labour. The manorial lord also exercised wide rights of government over his peasantry, levied taxes, and raised military forces when needed. Justice was administered by courts composed of the vassals of a common lord.

The feudal system prevailed in Europe from the tenth to the thirteenth century. Towards the end of this period it was undermined by a combination of various factors. The manorial system found itself in economic crisis, caused by rising prices and dwindling incomes of feudal lords. The revival of trade and growth of the towns contributed to the decline of the self-sufficient manor. The interests of the emergent merchant class clashed with those of the feudal lords; they consequently gave their support to the kings rather than to the barons. The lords, their vassals and private armies were gradually replaced by national states and a relationship of subject and sovereign. Nationalism developed fairly early in England and spread to the Continent, consolidating the position of the crown during the Hundred Years' War.

The medieval church also largely operated within the feudal system. The ecclesiastical offices held by bishops and abbots were endowed by the secular lords in return for homage, and carried with them property and revenues. The Church administered large revenues deriving from its landed estates, and from tithes and dues rendered by landowners and tenants. It thus wielded considerable temporal power, and enjoyed a large measure of independence and influence. The clergy were tried in church courts according to church law; the same applied to laymen in cases of heresy and sacrilege. A crucial factor contributing to the Church's authority was its dominance over education and culture within medieval society.

The Inquisition

The Inquisition was a papal judicial institution which dealt with heresy, witchcraft and sorcery. The medieval Inquisition, instituted by Pope Gregory IX in 1231, reserved to the Church the apprehension and trial of heretics, and was designed to combat certain specific heresies. It wielded greatest power in northern Italy and southern France in the thirteenth and fourteenth centuries; in the later Middle Ages it was mainly concerned with the trials of witches.

The papal inquisitors, who were often members of the Dominican order, were extremely powerful. Although most performed their duties with a regard for mercy, a few become renowned for cruelty. The use of torture to obtain confessions was authorised in 1252 by Innocent IV. Life imprisonment was the highest penalty the Inquisition could impose. Condemned heretics who refused to recant, or who relapsed, were turned over to the secular authorities for punishment.

The Spanish Inquisition was established in Spain by the Pope in the latter part of the fifteenth century. In general, its procedure was similar to the medieval Inquisition; but it gained a reputation for extreme cruelty and severity. The first grand inquisitor, the Dominican Tomas de Torquemada (1420–98), was notorious for his use of torture and terrorisation. Shaw may have had Torquemada in mind as a model for the Inquisitor in *Saint Joan*.

A note on the text

Saint Joan was first published in a single volume by Constable, London, in 1924. It was subsequently published, also by Constable, in the *Collected Edition* (1930–32) and *Standard Edition* (1937–49) of Shaw's works. The later *Complete Plays* was published by Odhams Press, London, and re-issued by Paul Hamlyn, London, 1965. Penguin Books published a paperback edition of *Saint Joan* in 1946; this edition has been reprinted many times. *Saint Joan* is included in vol. 6 of *The Bodley Head Bernard Shaw: Collected Plays with their Prefaces* (1933), edited by Dan H. Laurence, which has replaced the Standard Edition as the definitive authorised edition of Shaw's plays. Recent Penguin reprints are the paperback version of this definitive edition.

Shaw's screenplay for *Saint Joan* has been published by George Prior, New York, 1980, in *The Collected Screenplays of Bernard Shaw*, edited with an introduction by Bernard F. Dukore. No reference is made to this screenplay in these Notes.

Shaw required the printers of his plays to observe certain idiosyncratic usages of spelling, punctuation and typography. Apostrophes are omitted in contracted words such as 'isn't' or 'don't', unless there is a possibility of ambiguity. Shaw avoided the use of italics for emphasis in his dialogue, preferring to space the letters (as in 'y o u r', 'o n e'), and italicise only single-letter words ('*I*'). Titles of plays or books are not marked by quotation marks or italics (several examples occur in the Preface to *Saint Joan*). Shaw did however use italics for the lengthy settings and stage directions included in the published text. His idiosyncratic spelling includes some American forms, such as 'honor'. He also uses some American idioms such as 'gotten'.

The paperback edition of *Saint Joan* published by Penguin Books, Harmondsworth, 1946, has been used in the preparation of these Notes.

Part 2

Summaries
of SAINT JOAN

A general summary

The play begins in AD1429, during the Hundred Years' War between France and England. A young country girl has come to the castle of Vaucouleurs, to see the Squire. Captain Robert de Baudricourt is informed by his Steward that the girl refuses to return home despite his orders. De Baudricourt agrees to see the girl, who turns out to be Joan: she asks him to provide her with soldiers and horses, and to send her to the Dauphin. The Squire indignantly refuses Joan's request and dismisses her. However, Bertrand de Poulengey describes the power which Joan exerts over the soldiers, and suggests that her inspiration could help the French forces; moreover he is willing to pay for her horse. Joan is recalled, and on further questioning reveals that she hears voices from God, which instruct her to raise the siege of Orléans and crown the Dauphin in Rheims Cathedral. De Baudricourt is won over by Joan's persuasive eloquence and grants her request.

Joan goes to Chinon, to the Dauphin's court. The nobles and the Archbishop have little respect for the Dauphin, who is constantly in debt, and whose behaviour is hardly that of a king. Charles is excited at the prospect of Joan's imminent arrival, but the Archbishop at first attempts to prevent her from entering the court. When Joan is admitted, she successfully picks out the Dauphin from among a group of courtiers, and declares her mission to him. She overcomes the opposition of the court, and convinces Charles that he should assume full authority as King of France. Charles places her in command of the army, and the Archbishop gives her his blessing. Joan then proceeds towards Orléans, where she meets the French commander Jack Dunois on the south bank of the river. Joan declares that despite the superiority in numbers of the English forces, with God on her side she is certain of victory. Dunois points out that with an east wind blowing his men are unable to sail upstream and take the English from the rear. Suddenly the wind changes to a westerly direction: Dunois is convinced that Joan's mission is divinely inspired, and pledges her his loyalty. They set off to raise the siege.

Some time later, in the English camp, the Earl of Warwick and the English Chaplain meet the Bishop of Beauvais to discuss the problems posed by Joan's leadership and popularity. Since the siege of Orléans was raised the English have suffered further defeats. Warwick believes that Joan's support of the King poses a threat to feudal order, and Bishop Cauchon fears her challenge to the authority of the Church. Despite their differences they agree to oppose Joan as a common enemy. They agree on a plan whereby she will be captured by the English and handed over to the Church for trial as a heretic.

After Charles has been crowned in Rheims Cathedral, Joan announces that her mission is completed, and she intends to return home. She is distressed at her lack of support; indeed, most of the court, including Charles himself, are relieved at her decision. As Joan discusses with Dunois the next stage in the campaign to drive the English out of France, she changes her mind and decides to carry on fighting and take Paris. Dunois advises her that from now on the war will be tough, and warns that she can no longer rely for victory solely on the help of God. The Archbishop warns her that her pride and ambition point to a tragic downfall. It is clear, too, that if she is captured she cannot expect to be rescued by the army, the King or the Church. Despite all opposition, Joan resolves to go on to fight at Compiègne.

The next scene takes place in May 1431 in the castle at Rouen: Joan has been captured and handed over by the English to the Bishop's court for trial. Warwick is anxious that the proceedings should be brought to a speedy and satisfactory conclusion. However, the Inquisitor announces his decision to intervene and assume responsibility for Joan's trial. The ecclesiastical court assembles to hear the charges against Joan. When some of the assessors, notably the English Chaplain, protest that certain charges have been dropped, the Inquisitor explains that their concern should be with the main charge of heresy. He speaks at length of the dangers of heresy, and justifies the aims and methods of the Inquisition in dealing with it.

Joan is brought from prison before the court. When she refuses to take the oath of the Gospels, Courcelles, one of her assessors, demands that she be tortured; this request is refused by the Inquisitor. Bishop Cauchon asks Joan whether she will obey the Church's orders: she agrees, but only provided that such orders concur with the will of God, her voices and her own judgment. The court is shocked by this heretical view. Fresh charges are pressed against Joan, relating to her visions, and her soldier's dress. She refutes these charges. However, when the possibility of execution is put to her, Joan despairs of her voices, and agrees to sign a solemn recantation prepared by Martin Ladvenu. The Inquisitor declares her to be now free of heresy, but he sentences her to perpetual imprisonment. Horrified at this, Joan withdraws her recantation. She is solemnly excommunicated, and immediately led out to execution. Her piety and courage while being burnt at the stake impress both Martin Ladvenu and the English Chaplain de Stogumber. The

Executioner reports to Warwick that her remains have been thrown into the river according to his instruction, but that her heart would not burn.

Twenty-five years later the case of Joan is reconsidered, and the verdict of the earlier trial is overturned. At this point, in the Epilogue, the play takes on a fantastic, unrealistic quality. Ladvenu comes to King Charles's bedchamber to report that Joan has been rehabilitated. Charles is pleased, as this secures his royal status. The spirit of the dead Joan appears, followed by the ghost of Bishop Cauchon, who complains that he has been mistreated and vilified. Dunois then arrives, although he is actually asleep in his bed at Chateaudun: he also justifies his actions. A soldier who made a cross for Joan at the stake emerges briefly from hell. Chaplain John de Stogumber, now an elderly parish priest, recalls with horror the execution of Joan, but fails to recognise her ghost. The last figure to appear is a gentleman from the year 1920, who announces the Church's decision to canonise Joan. All kneel to praise Saint Joan. However, when she threatens to return to life, they are all alarmed at the prospect, and disappear one by one, leaving Joan alone.

Detailed summaries

The Preface

When his plays were published, either before or after they had been performed in public, Shaw wrote a Preface to be included in each volume. The Prefaces perform different functions. Sometimes they develop the themes and ideas of the play in a more coherent and extended argument. Alternatively, they may supply the historical or intellectual context for the story, or consider its implications for contemporary society. Shaw often used the Preface to present a cleverly argued defence of his position, following adverse criticism of the play in performance. Occasionally, the Preface relates to the drama in only a very general way. We must always be careful not to expect from the Preface a direct and straightforward commentary on the play, and we should avoid using it uncritically as a key to interpretation. In particular, Shaw's irony and his persuasive rhetoric are at work as much in the Prefaces as in the plays. However, this does not mean that we ought to ignore or dismiss the Preface. It may well be a useful and illuminating aside to the play, and will almost certainly be a valuable and thought-provoking essay in itself. It is safest, perhaps, to regard the Preface as a kind of postscript, directed towards Shaw's readers, but with a glance at the dramatic critics and the theatre audience. The Preface is thus obviously relevant to the play, but it is a separate and distinct piece of writing.

The Preface to *Saint Joan* uses as its focus the events which form the basis of the play, and discusses their historical significance and their relevance to the modern world. However, Shaw's air of authority and confidence in his writing should not mislead us into thinking this to be a purely factual account rather than a clever and elaborate argument. In addition, we should think carefully about whether or not the play actually dramatises the issues emphasised in the Preface in quite the way it suggests. As is usual with Shaw's Prefaces, it is divided into a number of sections under sub-headings. We may see the Preface as dealing with three main areas. First, Shaw analyses Joan's personality, and evaluates her motives and actions. He then examines her position in relation to the medieval Church, and the reasons for her excommunication, burning and subsequent rehabilitation. Finally, he accounts for the way in which he chose to shape her story into a drama, and answers objections which might be raised by critics.

The earlier sections, as far as 'Joan's Immaturity and Ignorance', deal with Joan's psychology, and the significance of her behaviour. Comparisons with Socrates and Napoleon pave the way for Shaw's assertion that Joan was a genius as well as a saint. It is wrong, he says, to emphasise Joan's appearance or treat her as a romantic heroine, as she was not conventionally feminine. It is also incorrect to regard her as a simple shepherdess; her social position as the daughter of a respected farmer was comfortable and secure. As for her voices and visions, Shaw compares these on the one hand to criminal delusions, and on the other to the intuitions and creative imagination of a genius. The voices are not supernatural in origin, although they might be called the manifestation of a force beyond the individual or the personal, driving the human race towards greater knowledge and power. Hallucinations are not to be dismissed as non-specific; they are a symbolic way of apprehending and representing reality, and are actually less superstitious than modern medicine or science. Nevertheless, their subjectivity is proved by their failure to advise Joan correctly over her rescue. Turning to Joan's desire to dress as a man, Shaw asserts that she, like some women in all ages, simply wished to lead a man's life. To sum up, Joan was sane, gifted and energetic, but her youth and inexperience inevitably brought her into conflict with authority.

After summarising the various accounts of Joan in literature Shaw turns, in 'Protestant Misunderstandings of the Middle Ages', to the historical context of her life. Her trial was no more or less fair than a comparable modern trial, although as an ecclesiastical trial it was of a special kind. It was inevitable, although tragic, that Joan's simple assertion of her private inspiration would lead to a clash with Church authority. The verdict was understandable, as was also the Church's later rehabilitation of Joan: once it was satisfied she was a saint, it could concede to her a special relationship with God. The burning of Joan was horrific, although not exceptionally cruel by medieval or modern standards. The Church should simply have excommunicated her, rather than put her to death. However, evolutionary progress such as that represented by Joan is always likely to appear to an average person as heresy or misconduct, so that society actually tends to suppress change. If originality and individuality are not tolerated, society will stagnate and eventually erupt into violence. The level of toleration varies according to circumstances such as national security, although recent events suggest that modern society is no more tolerant than that of the fifteenth century. The problem which Joan presented for her society lay in her issuing orders without explanation or justification except that she acted on God's authority. Such leadership can arouse either total obedience or extreme hostility, but it can only continue as long as things go well.

In the later sections of the Preface Shaw comments on his dramatisation of Joan's history. He has adapted the time scale for theatrical purposes, and elaborated on the available facts in order to develop dramatic characters. He has the advantage over Renaissance drama, and therefore over Shakespeare's dramatisation of Joan, of a clearer historical perspective. This has led him to reject the crude melodrama of Joan's persecution by evil men in favour of a more profound tragedy. In order to depict the essential truth, he has deliberately presented Cauchon in a favourable light. Shaw concludes by defending his play against the charge that it is too long and should be cut. The Epilogue is necessary to show the continuation of Joan's story after her death, and the overall duration of the performance, while it is unfashionably long for the London theatre, conforms to classical convention.

NOTES AND GLOSSARY:

Vosges:	mountainous area of Lorraine in France
Husites:	followers of John Hus, Bohemian religious reformer of the fifteenth century, burnt in 1415 (usual spelling 'Hussites')
plenipotentiary::	diplomatic agent invested with full powers
Church Triumphant:	community of the saints and those in heaven
pooh-poohed:	expressed contempt for
Cassius:	one of the Roman republic leaders responsible for the death of Julius Caesar in 44BC
Socrates:	Athenian philosopher of the fifth century (*d.* 399BC), whose writings on ethics gave rise to a number of schools of philosophy
Herod and Pilate:	Herod was tetrarch (ruler of a fourth part of a province) of Galilee, and Pontius Pilate governor of Judaea, at the time of Christ

Annas and Caiaphas: Jewish high priests in Jerusalem at the time of Christ

Jingo: crudely patriotic

Rationalist: philosopher who treats reason as the foundation of knowledge, and as the ultimate authority in religion as elsewhere

Byron's formula: quoted from Lord Byron's (1788−1824) *Don Juan* (1819−21), Canto I, stanza 194

Marie Antoinette: Austrian princess, queen of France (1755−93), executed during French revolution

Swedenborg: Emanuel Swedenborg (1688−1772), Swedish philosopher, natural scientist and mystic, who claimed divine authority to explain spiritual phenomena, and was chiefly known for his revolutionary scheme of Christian theology

Blake: William Blake (1757−1827), English Romantic poet

Pythagoras: Greek philosopher of sixth century BC, who held that the real nature of things is to be expressed in numbers; he also propounded the doctrine of transmigration of souls, and a cosmology close to that of Copernicus

Bedlamite: lunatic

Brocken spectres: optical illusions seen by an observer in an elevated position, when his shadow is projected on a cloud below; name derives from Brocken, a mountain in the Harz range

Materialist: one who holds the view that matter is the ultimate reality

Krishna: Hindu god, able to control natural elements

Louis Pasteur: French chemist and microbiologist (1822−95), originator of process known as pasteurisation which destroys pathogenic micro-organisms

Paul Bert: French politician and physiologist (1833−86), who worked on animal tissues and plant physiology

hagiology: literature dealing with lives and legends of saints

iconography: (study of) images of sacred personages

Galileo: Galileo Galilei (1564−1642), Italian mathematician, astronomer and physicist, founder of the experimental method

St Teresa: St Teresa of Avila

Edipus complex: in Freudian psychoanalysis, a son's unconscious sexual desire for his mother and his equally unconscious hatred for his father; name derived from

Oedipus (more usual spelling), who in ignorance of his own true identity killed his father and married his mother

adrenalin, thymin, pituitrin: glandular secretions or hormones

pre-Raphaelite movement: group of English artists of the nineteenth century, including Sir John Millais (1829–96) and Dante Rossetti (1828–82), who aimed to paint in the spirit that prevailed before the time of Raphael

Gardarene swine: see the New Testament, Matthew 8:28-33

Florence Nightingale: a famous reformer of nursing care in the Crimean War, who died in 1910

panjandrums: a mocking term for exalted officials

Armagnacs: the Armagnac district is in the south of France; the name Armagnacs was given to the party of the House of Orléans

Francis Galton: (1822–1911) British explorer, anthropologist and founder of the science of heredity and genetics

Rosa Bonheur: (1822–99) French painter, known for her studies of horses

George Sand: (1804–76) French novelist, real name Aurore Dupin, who had liaisons with Chopin and Liszt

Jerichowise: like Jericho, the town in Palestine whose wall, according to the Old Testament, fell at the sound of a trumpet

heresiarch: founder of heretical sect

Schiller: Friedrich von Schiller (1759–1805), German dramatist and poet who wrote *Die Jungfrau von Orleans* in 1801 as a corrective to Voltaire's account

Voltaire: the eminent French author (1694–1778), noted for his wit and satire

Pecksniffian: Pecksniff is a character in Charles Dickens's (1812–70) novel *Martin Chuzzlewit* (1844); the adjective is used to describe an unctuous hypocrite

Samuel Butler: English satirist (1835–1902), author of *The Way of All Flesh* (1903), and translator of the *Iliad* and the *Odyssey*

Agnes Sorel: mistress of Charles VII of France from 1444 to 1450, supposedly poisoned by the Dauphin (later Louis XI)

Quicherat: Quicherat's transcription of the trial of 1431 and subsequent rehabilitation proceedings of 1456 was translated by T. Douglas Murray in 1902

Mark Twain: pseudonym of the American writer Samuel

Clemens (1835–1910), author of *Personal Recollections of Joan of Arc* (1896)

Andrew Lang: Scottish scholar and man of letters (1844–1924), wrote the *Maid of France* (1908) as counterblast to the scepticism of Anatole France

Anatole France: French Socialist writer (1844–1924), wrote *La Vie de Jeanne d'Arc* (1908)

Bayard: (1475–1524) celebrated French knight and hero in Italian campaign of Charles VIII

Esther Summerson: the gentle, lovable heroine of Dickens's novel *Bleak House* (1853)

Albigensians: heretical sect at Albi, France, from twelfth century, which opposed Papal rule, and was put down with great cruelty by Innocent III

Edith Cavell: British nurse who worked in Belgium during the First World War, executed by a German firing squad in 1915 for conveying troops to the enemy

Roger Casement: Sir Roger Casement (1864–1916) was an Irish nationalist, who, after retiring from British consular service in 1913, joined the nationalist movement and visited Germany to seek assistance against the British; he was captured landing from a U-boat on the Kerry coast, convicted of treason and hanged in 1916; his remains were reburied in Ireland in 1965

Tommy and Jerry and Pitou: slang names for British, German and French soldiers

Sylvia Pankhurst: (1882–1960) a leading member of the suffragist movement, daughter of Emmeline Pankhurst who suffered nine times under the so-called 'Cat and Mouse Act', whereby a prisoner on hunger-strike could be released and re-arrested

Peculiar People: an evangelical Christian sect, founded in 1838 in London, which relied on divine intervention for cure of disease, and had no preachers or church organisation

Wycliffe: John Wycliffe (*c.* 1330–84), forerunner of Protestant Reformation

Mrs Eddy: Mary Baker Eddy (1821–1910), founder of the Church of Christ Scientist, which aims to cure disease by faith

Sidney and Beatrice Webb: English sociologists, founders of the London School of Economics and of *The New Statesman*

Richard Wagner: (1813–83); German composer of *Der Ring des Nibelungen*; Shaw wrote a treatise on Wagner's work, *The Perfect Wagnerite* (1891)

Calibanism: Robert Browning's (1812–89) poem *Caliban upon Setebos* (1855) is an expression of the crude philosophy of Caliban, the bestial figure who appears in Shakespeare's *The Tempest*

Laodiceanism: state of religious apathy, or indifference, like the Christians mentioned in the Bible, Revelations 3: 14–18

Ulster Orangeman: Protestant of Northern Ireland

Leicester Low Church: during rule of Elizabeth I, Lord Leicester, one of her ministers, staunchly supported Puritans

Henry Nevinson: English journalist and war correspondent, died 1941

Gallio: Roman proconsul of Achaia who refused, according to the New Testament, to try cases arising out of religious disputes, and dismissed the charges against St Paul

Machiavelli: Niccolo Machiavelli (1469–1527), Italian writer of political philosophy, author of the treatise *The Prince*

a step across the Rubicon: an irretrievable step; the Rubicon is a boundary, the passing of which commits one to an enterprise; derived from name of the stream limiting Caesar's province and separating Italy from Gaul, which he crossed before war with Pompey

Church Militant: community of Church on earth, engaged in constant struggle against evil

Apostolic Succession: theological doctrine maintaining uninterrupted transmission of spiritual authority through bishops from the Apostles downwards

Bruno: Giordano Bruno (1548–1600), author of metaphysical treatises, who strongly criticised Christianity

Freethinker: rejector of authority in religious belief

Vicar of Christ: the Pope

Ibsen's: Henrik Ibsen, Norwegian dramatist (1828–1906)

Abernethy: John Abernethy (1764–1831), English surgeon

Archbishop Laud: Archbishop of Canterbury, 1633–45, and influential statesman under Charles I, who was impeached by Cromwell and beheaded

Bulls of Pope Leo: Leo X (1513–21); in 1520 he issued a bull or papal edict excommunicating Luther

Butler's Erewhon: in Samuel Butler's utopia *Erewhon* (1901) illness is treated as a crime

Quakers: religious sect founded by George Fox in 1648, also known as the Society of Friends

Black and Tans: irregular force enlisted in 1920 for service in Ireland, whose original uniform was army khaki with black leather trappings

Star Chamber: room in the Palace of Westminster with ceiling covered in gilt stars, which was the seat of a tyrannical court under the early Stuarts

Habeas Corpus Act: in 1679, this Act made it illegal to hold a detainee indefinitely without trial

Defence of The Realm Act: the Act of August 1914 which provided the government with wide powers during the First World War

Garibaldi: Giuseppe Garibaldi (1807–82), Italian nationalist and patriot military leader of the movement for unification and independence

Betelgeuse: vivid red star in the constellation of Orion, with a diameter of two hundred million miles

Uffizi: an art gallery in Florence, founded by the Medicis in the fifteenth century

diabolus ex machina: (*Latin*) 'the devil from the machine'

deus ex machina: (*Latin*) 'the god from the machine', alluding to the machinery in the ancient theatre for bringing a god down upon the stage

Einstein: Albert Einstein (1879–1955), German mathematician and theoretical physicist who formulated special (1905) and general (1916) theories of relativity, and was awarded the Nobel prize for physics in 1922

Ober-Ammergau: a town in Bavaria where a pageant drama of Christ's Passion is performed every ten years

Aristotelian: Aristotle, the Greek philosopher (384–322BC), was the author of the *Poetics*, a famous treatise on tragedy

---

Scene I

It is a fine spring morning in the year 1429. The scene is set in the castle of Vaucouleurs, on the river Meuse between Lorraine and Champagne. Captain Robert de Baudricourt, squire of the castle, is scolding his steward because there are no eggs. The steward protests that it is not his fault: the hens will not lay, and the cows are giving less milk than usual.

He believes they have been bewitched by the Maid from Domrémy (who we learn later is Joan), who is still outside the castle despite having been told she cannot see the Squire. Robert is scornful of the steward's superstition, and even more angry that the girl has not yet been sent home to her father. The steward says that the girl simply will not go away. She spends all her time in the courtyard, talking to the soldiers and praying.

Robert shouts down to the girl to come upstairs. As soon as she comes in, she demands a horse, armour and soldiers, so she can go to the Dauphin Charles. Those, she says, are her orders from God. Robert is astounded at the Maid's directness and impudence, but finds it impossible to repress her. The Maid goes on to say that she will need three men. She already has the support of Bertrand de Poulengey, whom she refers to as Polly, and John of Metz, whom she calls Jack. She has arranged everything, and all Robert has to do is to give the order. Robert, amazed, calls for Polly, who tells him that all the soldiers respect the girl. He thinks her mission of going to the Dauphin may be worth a try. The situation is that the Duke of Burgundy and the English king have possession of half of France, including Paris. The Dauphin, uncrowned king of France, is trapped at Chinon, and it is likely that the English will capture the town of Orléans. Polly believes that only a miracle could save them, but Robert does not believe in miracles. De Poulengey agrees that it is a gamble to use the girl, but offers nevertheless to pay for her horse. This puts pressure on Robert to change his mind, and he decides to see Joan again.

Joan enters with the news that 'Jack', as she calls him, will pay half of the money needed for the horse. Robert asks Joan about her family and her age, and attempts to find out what she means by saying that St Catherine and St Margaret talk to her daily. Joan explains that she hears voices, which are the messages of God. These voices instruct her to raise the siege of Orléans, crown the Dauphin in the cathedral at Rheims, and make the English leave France. Robert tries to discourage her with alarming stories of the destruction wrought by the English soldiers and their commander the Black Prince, but Joan is not frightened. She believes that God is on her side, and that it is His will that the English should stay in their own country. By this time Joan has shown such determination that de Baudricourt changes his mind, thinking that she might after all be able to stir up the troops to fight. Accordingly he orders her to go to Chinon with an escort, and agrees to let her dress as a soldier. Joan goes out wildly excited, leaving de Baudricourt wondering whether she has made a fool of him. The steward runs in to say that the hens have started laying. Robert, startled by this turn of events, takes it as evidence of Joan's supernatural powers. He is converted into believing that she was indeed sent by God.

NOTES AND GLOSSARY:

a military squire:	soldier and landowner
mullioned:	(of a window) divided into sections, usually by vertical stone bars
your Maker:	God
jibbering:	more usually written 'gibbering'
Barbary:	old name for North Africa
men-at-arms:	armed guard
Be you captain?:	Are you the Captain? This ungrammatical usage is Shaw's way of indicating that Joan speaks in local dialect. De Baudricourt copies her when he says 'I be captain'
blockhead:	(*slang*) an unintelligent person
francs:	a franc is the unit of French currency
baggage:	slang term for a woman, common in nineteenth-century English. Shaw is often deliberately anachronistic in his use of colloquialisms
dithering:	literally 'vacillating', but here used loosely as a deprecatory adjective
lymphatic:	flabby, sluggish
gentleman-at-arms:	one of the bodyguards of a sovereign or lord
wench:	girl, lass
bourgeoise:	member of the middle, rather than working class; an anachronism, as the term is more properly applied to post-feudal society
humbugging:	deluding
no end of a mess:	serious trouble; colloquial expression
her father's lord:	feudal lord
down and out:	beaten; a colloquialism derived from the rules of boxing
take:	capture
leave any stone unturned:	neglect to try any possible means
precious:	a colloquial intensifier
choke you:	beat you
Black Prince:	Edward, Prince of Wales (1330–76), eldest son of Edward III of England
goddams:	English soldiers; as Robert explains, this slang word is a corruption of 'God damn'
plumping down:	sitting down abruptly and heavily
encircled with lights, like a saint's:	Joan means that she sees a halo round his head
I wash my hands of it:	I deny any responsibility
to boot:	in addition
like mad:	in great quantities

Scene II

The scene is set in an antechamber of the throne room of the castle of Chinon, late in the afternoon of 8 March 1429. The Archbishop of Rheims and the Lord Chamberlain, Monseigneur de la Trémouille, are waiting for the Dauphin; the latter is angry that the Dauphin is late; he also complains that Charles owes him a great deal of money. It seems that Charles is habitually in debt to his lords. Another member of the court, Gilles de Rais, known as Bluebeard, enters with the news that Foul Mouthed Frank has fallen into a well and drowned, shortly after an unknown soldier reproved him for swearing when he was on the point of death. This striking incident has alarmed Captain La Hire, who is also given to swearing, and who has found out that the unknown soldier is female and, he says, an angel. At this point the Dauphin is announced. He proves to be unimpressive in appearance, and petulant and self-centred in disposition. It is clear that his courtiers have little respect for him. Just now the Dauphin is excited by a letter he has received from Robert de Baudricourt, who is sending to him his own personal saint (or holy personage), dressed in armour. La Hire realises that this is the same soldier who reprimanded Foul Mouthed Frank. The courtiers are unwilling for the Maid to be admitted, and the Archbishop forbids it. However, they are interested to hear from the letter that she intends to raise the siege of Orléans, and all, including the Archbishop, eventually relent. The Dauphin and Bluebeard go off to arrange a test of Joan's powers by putting Bluebeard in Charles's place, to see if she will recognise the true Dauphin. The Lord Chamberlain thinks that this will be a difficult challenge; the Archbishop, who is less credulous and more sceptical, assumes that Joan will succeed by straightforward deduction. Indeed, the Archbishop considers that such 'miracles' are a mixture of common sense and simple contrivance, but they conform with the nature and purpose of miracles as he understands them: that is, as events which create faith.

The curtains of the throne room are drawn back to reveal the court fully assembled. Bluebeard is pretending to be the Dauphin, and Charles mingles inconspicuously with the courtiers. When Joan comes in she quickly sees through the trick, and recognises both Bluebeard and Charles. She announces her mission to the Dauphin and kneels in reverence to the Archbishop. They are both pleased by the special attention and respect which she, unlike others in the court, pays to them. However, the Archbishop knows that her excessive religious fervour could be dangerous. Joan's appearance and manner cause some mirth among the courtiers and their ladies; their ridicule is upbraided by the Archbishop and by Joan herself.

Joan asks to be allowed to speak to the Dauphin alone. She urges

Charles to assume much greater responsibility as king, by being crowned, and by leading the fight against the English. Charles has no wish to be king; he lacks courage and determination and wants only to lead a quiet life and conclude a treaty with the English. However, he is unable to resist Joan's enthusiasm and eloquence. In his excitement, he recalls the court and announces that he is giving full command of the army to the Maid. La Trémouille, who was previously the commander, is displeased; but the court, like Charles, is inspired by Joan, and the Archbishop finally gives her his blessing.

NOTES AND GLOSSARY:

Lord Chamberlain: high-ranking court official, usually responsible for the management of a royal household

wineskin of a man: a man large and fleshy from too much drinking; a wineskin is a whole skin of an animal such as a goat, sewn up and used to hold wine

cool: slang term used (of large sums of money) as an intensifier

no shadow of the gallows: nothing to suggest that he will subsequently be hanged

faithful lamb: a member of the Church flock, a devoted Christian

put my foot down: take up a firm position

saint: in this instance, a living person of great holiness

cracked: crazy

war dog: a typical military man, accustomed to fighting

blackguard: scoundrel, foul-mouthed person

excommunication matter: a fault incurring the severest punishment by the Church

Rot!: (*slang*) nonsense!

a blazing ass: (*slang*) a conspicuous fool

spunk: courage

fishy: questionable

Man alive: a colloquial expletive

humbug: fraud, deceitful nonsense

artful fox: cunning person

Consort: wife or husband of a ruler

halberd: a weapon, a combined spear and battle-axe

Coom: dialect representation of 'Come'

on the broad grin: smiling broadly

may as well be hanged for a sheep as a lamb: proverbial expression meaning that if punishment is inevitable, there is no point in restricting one's criminal activity

Gruff-and-Grum: Joan is referring to La Trémouille's surly, ill-tempered speech; Grum = grumpy

magnetic field:	the force of Joan's personality; a magnetic field is the region of influence of a magnet
St Louis:	Louis IX, King of France from 1226
save your breath to cool your porridge:	keep your advice and instruction for your own use
Blethers!:	nonsense!
noddle:	(*colloquial*) head
pawnshop:	place of business of a pawnbroker, who lends money for interest on security of personal property left as a pledge with him
Judas:	the disciple who betrayed Jesus
gauntlet:	armed glove

Scene III

On the south bank of the river Loire, close to Orléans, Jack Dunois is lamenting the lack of a west wind which prevents his troops from sailing upstream to attack the English forces. It is the evening of 29 April. Dunois and his page watch the kingfisher darting about in the reeds, while they wait for the wind to change and for the Maid to arrive. Joan rushes in dressed in armour, furious to find she has been brought as she thinks to the wrong side of the river, away from Orléans and the English. Dunois explains to Joan that the forts on the bridge are unassailable, but she declares that she would nevertheless tackle them without fear. Her courage and faith defy such obstacles. It would be more strategic, according to Dunois, to approach the forts from the rear by water; however, the boats are held downstream by the east wind. Before she can prove herself as a soldier, Dunois suggests, Joan must pray for a west wind. As they are about to leave for the church, the page sneezes, and at once realises that the flag is now streaming the other way. The wind has changed direction, as if in anticipation of Joan's prayers. Dunois sees this as a sign from God, and pledges loyalty to Joan. The boats have already set sail upstream, and Joan and Dunois set off in a state of exhilaration to capture the forts.

NOTES AND GLOSSARY:

pennon:	long narrow flag
bend sinister:	heraldic device indicating illegitimacy
strumpet:	wanton woman
kingfisher:	small bird with brilliant blue-green plumage, usually found close to a river bank, feeding on the fish which it captures by diving
Mary:	the Virgin Mary
snood:	a net hair covering
fat-heads:	dolts, fools

mettle: spirit, courage, quality of disposition
breach of promise: breaking of promise to marry
sally: a sudden rush by way of surprise attack
ripping: rushing along
capers: leaps

Scene IV

In a tent in the English camp the Earl of Warwick awaits a visit from
the Bishop of Beauvais, to discuss how the authorities are to rid themselves of Joan. Warwick disagrees with the chaplain, John de Stogumber, over the seriousness of the English position. The siege of Orléans
has been raised, and the English have also been defeated at Jargeau,
Meung and Beaugency. Following a further defeat at Patay, their commander Sir John Talbot has been captured. The Chaplain attributes
the successive defeats to witchcraft practised by Joan. He is anxious
that she should be destroyed. The Earl of Warwick regards the defeat
as a temporary set-back which will be overcome by making a deal with
the other side to destroy Joan's power.

When the Bishop of Beauvais, Monseigneur Cauchon, arrives, neg-
otiations commence. Warwick proposes that the Church should burn
Joan as a witch, but Cauchon doubts whether a church court would
actually convict her of sorcery. The Chaplain is outraged by what he
takes to be a lenient view of Joan's evil practices; however, Cauchon
goes on to explain that he regards her sin as even more serious than that
of sorcery. It is the sin of heresy, which could damn Joan's soul and
threaten the authority of the Catholic Church, and which marks her as
being inspired by the devil. Nevertheless, the Bishop cannot guarantee
that she will be burnt: first, because the Church will seek to save Joan's
soul rather than simply condemn her; and secondly, because the
Church itself would not actually execute her, but would hand her over
to the secular authorities for sentence and punishment. At this point it
seems that there is a fundamental clash of interests and objectives between Cauchon and Warwick, Church and State, French and English,
which is about to erupt into an angry conflict. However, Warwick
diplomatically soothes the Bishop's anger, and they proceed to discuss
further how their common interests can be met with regard to Joan.
They are agreed at least that her continued liberty, and even her life,
are a problem to both of them.

The Chaplain wonders how Joan can be condemned as a heretic,
since she appears to be so pious. This angers Cauchon, who equates
Joan with the spread of heresy in Bohemia and in England. The heresy
of direct individual divine inspiration leads men to set themselves up as
prophets and leaders. The Bishop sees in such figures the threat of dis-

ruption and chaos. The Earl of Warwick is less concerned at the threat which Joan poses to the Church, than at the threat which her attitude to the Dauphin poses to feudal aristocracy and thus to the stability of society. Her emphasis on the power of the king makes him absolute master, rather than one among a number of noblemen. This in turn threatens the relation of the feudal lords to their own people.

It is clear that the Church and State have different things to fear from Joan. However, Cauchon urges that they unite against Joan as a common enemy. Warwick agrees that the central issue is the rebellion of the individual against authority, whether of Church or State; he calls Joan's religious attitude Protestantism, and Cauchon names her political stance Nationalism. The Chaplain does not understand these categories; nevertheless, Joan rebels against what he holds to be natural and right – against the Church, God and England. He insists that she must be burnt, whereas the Bishop will continue to seek her salvation, and even Warwick would spare her life if possible. They are united, however, in wanting her to be removed from power.

NOTES AND GLOSSARY:

illuminated Book of Hours: book containing prayers to be said at appointed times, and decorated with small paintings

cassock: long tunic worn by clergy

Holy Land: Palestine, especially Judaea

Burgundians and Bretons and Picards and Gascons: inhabitants of these various regions of France

the Conqueror: William I of England, Duke of Normandy, known as William the Conqueror, who invaded England and defeated the English king at Hastings in 1066

One has to leave a margin: provide for a profitable transaction. In this speech Shaw makes Warwick speak as if getting hold of Joan were a commercial deal. The Chaplain's reference to Jews is an allusion to the developing financial systems of European capitalism, with Jews often lending capital on security and on payment of interest

Messire: title and form of address; compare Monseigneur, Monsieur

drab: slut

Beelzebub: a name for the devil

trumpery imp: worthless little devil

Prince of Darkness: Satan

grow a very thick skin: become impervious to emotional shock

A beggar on horseback!: a pretentious person

an Arab camel driver: Mahomet

ravaged his way west: refers to the spread of the Muslim religion

Mother of God: the Virgin Mary

keystone to the arch: used figuratively to mean a central organising principle of society

Will to Power: the phrase originates from the German philosopher Friedrich Nietzsche (1844–1900), who postulated the will to power as the basic principle of all existence

the pink of: the perfection of

Sancta simplicitas!: (*Latin*) Holy simplicity! While about to be burned at the stake John Hus exclaimed this when an old peasant woman threw more wood onto the pile, thinking she was serving God by helping to burn a heretic

---

Scene V

Charles has been crowned king in the cathedral at Rheims. After the coronation Joan is kneeling in prayer. Dunois urges her to show herself to the people who are clamouring to see her, but despite her courage in battle, Joan fears such a public ordeal. She cannot understand the hostility shown towards her by the courtiers, knights and churchmen, and admits to Dunois that only the voices which she hears give her the determination to go on.

Charles, now anointed as king, enters, complaining about the arduous coronation ceremony. He receives with equanimity Joan's announcement that she is going back to her father's farm. Indeed, no-one tries to persuade her to stay. Suddenly she changes her mind, and entreats Dunois to join her in capturing Paris before she goes home. Charles does not approve; he would prefer a treaty with Burgundy. Joan vehemently insists that she is right, whereupon the Archbishop warns her against the sin of pride which, he says, could lead to her downfall. Joan claims the authority and sanction of her voices on this issue, adding that it would in any case be sensible to capture Paris. La Hire agrees with her, but Dunois is more cautious and stresses the importance of careful military strategy. Joan is scornful of the medieval art of war with its rules and conventions which Dunois represents; she will rely only on gunpowder, strength of arms and her own powers of leadership. Dunois still maintains that her total trust in God is over-confident, and that she takes unnecessary risks with small forces of men. He predicts that she will be captured, and moreover that the French army will do nothing to save her.

No more support is forthcoming for Joan from either Charles or the Archbishop. The Archbishop points out that a woman has already been burnt as a witch for supporting her. Joan believes that the Church must protect her. However, the Archbishop states clearly that the

Church will not defend her in her stubborn insistence on setting her own judgment, ratified by the voices which she hears, above the authority of the Church, or the advice of the military or the king. The penalty of her faith in her privilege of hearing voices from God is to stand absolutely alone and unsupported. There is no point in her trusting to the acclaim of the crowd, who will not save her. Joan rejects the Archbishop's advice to compromise with authority, although she recognises her isolated position. She will trust only in her special relationship with God, rejecting temporal and spiritual authorities even if it costs her her life.

Joan goes out to show herself to the ordinary people, seeking comfort in their display of devotion. The others are left behind, glum and dispirited at her intransigence. Bluebeard and Dunois still admire and like her, but feel they cannot prevent her from destroying herself. La Hire finds the force of her personality irresistible, and the Archbishop too recognises its power. He also sees that Joan is on the edge of disaster, impelled towards her own doom.

NOTES AND GLOSSARY:

ambulatory: cloister

vestry: room in which vestments are kept and put on

stations of the cross: series of fourteen images or pictures representing Christ's passion, before which devotions are performed

dug-outs: (*colloquial*) elderly persons returning to work after long retirement, bringing back obsolete ideas

take his hand from the plough: stop working

hubris: a term used in relation to Greek tragedy, denoting overweening pride which offends the gods and leads to nemesis

angelus: devotional exercise commemorating the annunciation of the incarnation to the Virgin Mary, and said in the morning, at noon and sunset at the sound of the bell. The opening words are 'Angelus domini'

If ifs and ans . . . : proverbial phrase; Joan means that it is futile to wait for the right conditions

Caesar: title given to the rulers of Rome (after Julius Caesar (100BC–44BC)) from Augustus (63BC–AD14) to Hadrian (AD76–138)

Caesar and Alexander: Bluebeard means that Joan is determined to adopt the power of an autocrat, depending for political and military supremacy on sole authority over the people.

of Agincourt, of Poitiers and Crecy: these were all battles in the Hundred Years' War between French and English

Scene VI

It is the morning of 30 May 1431. The scene is set in the castle of Rouen,
when the great hall is arranged as a court-room. The Earl of Warwick
enters with his page, who points out that his master has no authority
over this ecclesiastical court. Warwick, however, wishes to speak to the
Bishop of Beauvais before the trial begins. The Bishop comes in,
accompanied by the Inquisitor and the Promoter or prosecutor. Warwick demands to know what stage the proceedings have reached, as it is
now nine months since Joan was captured, and her trial has continued
for eleven weeks. The Inquisitor explains that he has just decided that
this is a case of heresy which must be heard by the Holy Inquisition, not
merely the Bishop's court. This stage of the trial is about to begin.
Warwick is anxious for a judgment, and holds that the Maid's death is
a political necessity. The churchmen are concerned that she should
have a fair hearing; however, the Inquisitor and Promoter feel sure she
will condemn herself by what she says.

Warwick leaves, and the full court assembles. The Bishop's assessors
include Chaplain de Stogumber and a young French priest, Canon de
Courcelles. These two protest that the charges against Joan have been
drastically reduced, omitting for example her statement that the saints
spoke to her in French, and her alleged theft of the Bishop of Senlis's
horse. Cauchon is rather flustered by their objections, but the Inquisitor intervenes to emphasise that the main issue is Joan's heresy. The
court of the Inquisition should not concern itself with slighter charges
which might prove irrelevant. When Brother Martin Ladvenu questions the seriousness of Joan's heresy, the Inquisitor speaks at length to
the court about the grave threat which it poses. Such heresy may start
in apparent innocence and even piety but it develops into immorality
and unnatural wickedness. The Inquisition is used to dealing with
claims of divine inspiration which are sincerely and honestly believed
by the heretics, such as Joan, who claim them. He warns the court to
guard against natural compassion, although he is not advocating unjust
harshness. He maintains, however, that even the severest punishment
of the Inquisition is less cruel than the violent response of the common
people to heretics, and may actually save life if the heretic repents. The
Inquisition is right, necessary and essentially merciful. Accordingly he
instructs the court to proceed to a fair trial, with justice as the first consideration. At the end of this long speech Cauchon declares that he
shares the opinion of the Inquisitor. He adds that the most dangerous
heresy, and one that is increasingly prevalent, is what the Earl of Warwick has called Protestantism.

Joan, chained by the ankles, is now brought in and led to the prisoner's stool. She complains that the prison food has made her ill, and

that her feet are chained to a log. The young priest Courcelles interjects that when she was unchained, she tried to escape by jumping from the tower. Joan thinks it only natural to try to escape, although to the Promoter this implied refusal to place herself in the hands of the Church amounts to heresy. At this point the Inquisitor stresses that the court's proceedings must be formally opened, with Joan swearing on the Gospels to tell the whole truth. Joan, however, will not tell the whole truth; nor will she swear. Courcelles interrupts again to demand that she be tortured, and the Executioner (who is also the torturer) confirms that the instruments are ready. Joan objects that she can always say what she likes under torture, and recant later. Ladvenu seizes on this to advocate leniency, and despite Courcelles's continued pleas for torture as the correct and customary procedure, the Inquisitor and the Bishop decide that careful questioning is to be preferred.

Cauchon then puts to Joan the solemn question of whether she is prepared to accept the judgment of the Church regarding her voices and revelations, and her unconventional conduct. Joan answers that she must obey God's commands, even if this means going against the Church. The court is shocked at the implication that it is possible for the Church's commands to be contrary to God's word. As Cauchon warns, this is heresy. The Inquisitor then presses Joan to accept that her visions are sent by the devil to tempt her. However Joan insists that she has simply followed the commands of God in the matters that he refers to as crimes. Brother Martin tries to save her from condemning herself, by making her admit that she is subject to the Church, but Joan still finally places God and her own judgment first. This convinces the court that she is a heretic.

The Bishop is impatient when more trivial questions are raised by Courcelles. The Promoter nevertheless emphasises the gravity of the two further charges of intercourse with evil spirits and of wearing men's clothes. Joan will not accept that her apparitions are evil spirits. Moreover, she regards it as common sense to dress as a soldier when she is with soldiers; far from being immoral, it may help to safeguard her chastity. It now seems that no efforts to save Joan will succeed, despite Ladvenu's attempts to make the best of her simple and direct answers. Joan is unaware that she has said anything wrong, and is scornful of the learned wisdom of the court. Ladvenu warns that preparations have been made to burn her as a heretic, with hundreds of soldiers gathered outside. The Executioner confirms that the stake is ready in the market place. Joan, on the point of despair, cannot believe that her voices would lead her into such danger. She is persuaded by Cauchon and Brother Martin that she has been deceived, and declares herself ready to recant. The English Chaplain, angry that Joan is to escape burning, accuses the French of treachery. Meanwhile Ladvenu has prepared a solemn recantation for Joan to sign. By it she is to confess that she has pretended to have divine visitations; that she has blasphemed by dressing immodestly; and that she has committed the sins of sedition, idolatry, disobedience, pride and heresy. Henceforth she is to renounce her sins and remain obedient to the Church. When Joan has made her mark in lieu of signature of the recantation, the Inquisitor declares her free from the danger of excommunication. However, she must do penance by remaining in solitary confinement for the rest of her life. Joan is shocked and angry. Lifelong imprisonment is to her a worse punishment than death, and the severity of this sentence proves to her that her judges are evil.

The Promoter declares Joan to be a relapsed heretic, and calls for her excommunication. Encouraged by the Chaplain, the Executioner hurries out to light the fire at the stake. Joan's final statement is that it is the will of God that she should be put to death. Cauchon and the Inquisitor formally intone a solemn decree of excommunication, relinquishing her to the secular authorities for punishment. Before she can be officially handed over to the Earl of Warwick, she is rushed out to the courtyard by the Chaplain. Ladvenu hastens to be with her. As the flickering of the fire is seen in the courtyard, the Bishop makes to go out and stop the execution. However, the Inquisitor points out that the court has proceeded correctly, and no blame will fall on them if the English put themselves in the wrong. After all, the sooner it is over the better for Joan. The Bishop is surprised when the Inquisitor proclaims Joan's innocence; she has simply been caught up in complicated issues which she could not understand.

As the Bishop and the Inquisitor turn to go out, Warwick enters. Cauchon remembers that Warwick's men have not observed the forms of law, while Warwick casts doubt on the Bishop's authority outside his own diocese. There is unconcealed hostility between the two men, as Warwick is left alone. He calls for an attendant, but it is the Chaplain who staggers in from the courtyard howling and sobbing. He has been shocked and distressed at seeing how terrible death by burning was. He is now convinced that Joan has found salvation; when she was surrounded by flames, she cried to Jesus. When she asked for a cross, a soldier tied two sticks together. The Chaplain thinks this must have been an English soldier; and those who laughed must have been French. Ladvenu returns, not distraught like the Chaplain but serious and composed. He is convinced that Joan was indeed close to God, and predicts that her death will not end the matter. Stogumber rushes out in despair; and Warwick urges Ladvenu to guard him. The Executioner arrives to report to Warwick that his orders have been carried out: Joan's remains have been thrown into the river, so that there will be no relics. Her heart, he reports, would not burn.

NOTES AND GLOSSARY:

canons:	clergy, members of the cathedral chapter
Dominican monks:	members of an order of preaching friars, named after its founder, St Dominic (1170–1221)
secular arm:	civil jurisdiction
brief:	summary of a law-case
Chapter:	group of church officers who look after the affairs of a cathedral
vulpine:	of the nature of a fox, cunning
Holy Office:	the Inquisition
Apostolic Succession:	theological doctrine of uninterrupted transmission of spiritual authority through bishops since the time of the Apostles
Moab:	region east of Dead Sea in Jordan
Ammon:	region east of river Jordan, north of Moab
noodle:	simpleton
surcoat:	loose coat worn over armour
St Athanasius:	bishop of Alexandria for forty-five years from AD328, whose name is attached to a version of the Creed (brief formal summary of Christian doctrine, recited as a confession of faith)
the shepherd rejoices ... :	see the Bible, Luke 15:7
antiphonally:	alternately, like the verses of a psalm intoned or sung as responses by alternating choirs during a church service
makes a feint of:	pretends to
runs:	is valid

Epilogue

Charles is reading in bed in one of his chateaux on a windy night in June 1456. Brother Martin Ladvenu enters, still carrying the cross from Rouen, to inform Charles that the recent inquiry into Joan's trial twenty-five years earlier is now concluded. Ladvenu denounces the proceedings of this inquiry as corrupt, yet admits they have revealed the truth about Joan. She has been cleared of witchcraft and heresy, while her judges at the earlier trial have been pronounced malicious and corrupt. Charles is pleased at this outcome, because it makes his coronation by Joan valid and respectable, and his own position secure.

When Ladvenu has left, a sudden rush of wind fills the room. (This marks the beginning of the strange and supernatural events, and the movement of the action of the play away from theatrical realism.) The figure of Joan is seen dimly in a greenish light by Charles's bedside. Charles tells her what has been happening since they last met. He now leads his soldiers into battle as a brave king, and he has loved a young woman called Agnes Sorel. He also informs Joan that the sentence on her has been annulled, and her memory will now be sacred.

Bishop Cauchon appears at the window. He too is dead; after his death he was excommunicated, and his body exhumed and flung into a sewer. He feels this dishonour to be a blow struck against the Church. Moreover, he will be remembered as a figure of evil and cruelty, although he was in fact sincere and faithful to his conscience. At this point Jack Dunois comes through the tapestry. He is not dead, but his spirit is temporarily separated from his sleeping body. Since Joan died he has beaten the English and driven them out of France. The next to arrive is the English soldier who made a cross for Joan out of two sticks. He is released from hell for one day each year because of his good deed, and is free until midnight. Surprisingly, he reports that hell is not after all a place of torment. Moreover, he has the company of emperors and popes.

A gentle knocking is heard, and Chaplain de Stogumber appears. He is now a white-haired old priest, rector of a village parish. It is clear that the shock of seeing Joan burned to death had a deep and long-lasting effect on him. De Stogumber does not recognise Joan. However, the Executioner, stepping from behind the bed curtains, sees that her spirit lives on. The Earl of Warwick, also appearing from behind the bed curtains, congratulates Joan on her rehabilitation. He apologises for his part in her execution, but considers that by it he contributed to her being made a saint.

At this point, a gentleman who looks rather like a clergyman appears in the corner. He is wearing the dress of 1920, and the others find his appearance strange and ridiculous. The gentleman reads out an offical pronouncement that Joan of Arc has been canonised as Saint Joan. Joan is overwhelmed and humbled at this news. Visions of statues erected to her in the cathedrals at Winchester and Rheims are seen. As they fade, the figures of the Archbishop and the Inquisitor appear on the right and left of Cauchon. All kneel to Joan and recite a catalogue of praise, from all the members of the community whom they represent and for whom she can provide comfort and inspiration. This makes Joan rather uncomfortable. She asks if she should return from the dead, if they are all so devoted to her. They are all extremely dismayed at such a prospect, and one by one they excuse themselves and vanish. It seems that her return to life would be an awkward embarrassment. Eventually only the soldier remains. He thinks their behaviour is typical of rulers and professional people, and prepares to talk at length on this topic. However, a distant bell strikes midnight, and he has to return once more to hell. Left alone, Joan wonders when the world will be able to understand and accept people such as herself.

NOTES AND GLOSSARY:

lancet window: tall narrow window with pointed top in Gothic buildings

Fouquet's Boccaccio: Jean Fouquet (*c.* 1420–80), French painter of miniatures to illustrate books, including Boccaccio

Boccaccio: Italian writer (1313–75), author of the *Decameron*, a collection of a hundred short stories

Charlemagne: Charles the Great (742–814), King of the Franks (from 768) and emperor (from 800)

King David: King of Israel (*d.* 1000BC)

say that top-side-up is right-side-up: Charles means that he accepts the usual and conventional way of looking at things

keep my nose pretty close to the ground: behave conventionally and inconspicuously

chaffering: bargaining

give you best: admit your superiority, admit you were right

Church Militant: the community of the Church on earth, engaged in constant struggle against evil

Church Triumphant: the community of the saints and those in heaven, who have conquered evil

Rum tum trumpledum . . . : as the soldier says later, this is nonsense verse

doggrel: doggerel, trivial or unpolished verse

troubadour: lyric poet of the type originating in Provence in the eleventh century AD

Tip top: the very best

chip me: (*colloquial*) make fun of me

judy: (*slang*) girl

chanty: variant of 'shanty'

howler: glaring blunder

frockcoat: a man's long-skirted coat, usually of fine black cloth, worn as respectable day-wear in nineteenth and early twentieth centuries, subsequently worn only on formal ceremonial occasions

Venerable and Blessed: titles relating to successive stages in the process of canonisation

Mercy Seat: throne of God in Heaven

Anglican heresy: the Church of England may be so described by Roman Catholics; the Gentleman's remark reminds us that he is of the twentieth century, and so post-Reformation, whereas the other characters belong to the fifteenth century

Part 3

Commentary

Historical drama of the nineteenth century

During the nineteenth century historical drama was an extremely popular theatrical form. Extravagant spectacle was a prominent feature of the plays of James Robinson Planché (1796–1880) and others. The choice of an historical subject provided playwrights and managers with the opportunity for a lavish display of costumes and splendid pageantry, under the pretext of a serious concern for accuracy of contemporary detail. Elaborate stage effects, such as the proscenium arch, solid stage sets and electric lighting, were made possible by technical advances which increased theatrical illusion. The style of the plays was highly rhetorical, often using ornate, formal and poetic speeches. Some, like Lord Tennyson's (1809–92) *Becket* (1884), were actually written in verse. In both pageantry and style the historical dramas were influenced by Shakespeare's tragedies and histories, which in the nineteenth century were presented in truncated, vulgarised versions, again with an eye for spectacle.

The plots were often built around a romantic interest (the novels of Sir Walter Scott (1771–1832) were adapted for the stage). Major historical events and famous figures became the background to romance, either fictitious or genuine, as in Tom Taylor's (1817–80) *Lady Clancarty; or, Wedded and Wooed, A Tale of the Assassination Plot, 1696* (1874). There were, however, also plays which focused on the lives of notable historical figures, such as *Richelieu* (1839) by Lord Bulwer-Lytton (1803–73), or *Louis XI* (1855) by Dion Boucicault (?1820–90). In general, historical drama of the nineteenth century presented pageantry and poetry on a base of romantic melodrama. Melodrama influenced the plots and characterisation, with a simple moral and dramatic scheme of distress and rescue, and heroes whose qualities and virtues were greatly exaggerated. The starring role invited magnificent acting and extravagant histrionics, and so provided an attractive vehicle for the great actor-managers such as Sir Henry Irving (1870–1919), who played in Tennyson's verse drama *Becket*. Plays were also written to provide star parts for the great actresses, with heroines equivalent to the male roles of Shakespeare and the contemporary history plays. The plays used for this purpose include *Maria Stuart* (1801) by Schiller, *Marie Antoinette* (1804) by the Italian popular dramatist

Giacomnetti (1816–82) (an historical pageant like *Saint Joan*), and Tom Taylor's *Jeanne Darc (Called the Maid); a Chronicle Play, in Five Acts* (1871), which Shaw may have seen in Dublin. While he lived in Dublin Shaw also had the chance to see such female stars as Adelaide Ristori, Kate Bateman and Ada Cavendish, and was particularly impressed by Madame Ristori's grand style. Historical drama was also familiar to him from the London theatre. His collected dramatic criticism, *Our Theatres in the Ninties*, includes a review of the Lyceum production of Victorien Sardou's (1831–1908) *Madame Sans-Gêne* (1893), with Ellen Terry and Henry Irving. This play about Napoleon may have influenced his own historical drama *The Man of Destiny*. Much later, he saw Sybil Thorndyke, the actress whom he chose to play Saint Joan, in a performance of Percy Bysshe Shelley's (1792–1822) historical verse drama *The Cenci* (1819).

Shaw's history plays

Historical settings and themes are found in a number of Shaw's plays, including *The Man of Destiny* (1895), *The Devil's Disciple* (1897), *Caesar and Cleopatra* (1899), *Androcles and the Lion* (1912), *The Dark Lady of the Sonnets* (1910), *Great Catherine* (1913) and *In Good King Charles's Golden Days*. The most important of these as historical dramas are *The Man of Destiny* (1895) and *Caesar and Cleopatra* (1899). Each play deals with a famous historical figure, Napoleon and Caesar respectively (both of whom Shaw compares with Joan in the Preface to *Saint Joan*). *The Man of Destiny* is subtitled 'A Fictitious Paragraph of history', and the action hinges on a small incident which is supposed to have occurred during the Italian campaign of 1796, when military despatches addressed to Napoelon are intercepted by a mysterious lady. The duel of wits in which these two main characters engage for possession of the papers has overtones of the battle of the sexes. The plot of *The Man of Destiny*, involving as it does intrigue, disguise and clandestine love affairs, is in the vein of historical romance; but its theme is the gap between the notion of romantic heroism and the realities of leadership and power. Shaw wrote the play after he had seen *Madame Sans-Gêne*, as an attempt to correct what he considered to be a misconceived characterisation of Napoleon by Sardou. Shaw's Napoleon is shown not as a hero governed by high ideals of honour and truth, but as a shrewd, pragmatic and professional campaigner. Nevertheless, although the play dispels romantic illusions, it presents Napoleon as the true Shavian hero, as a realist and a vitalist. It is in fact a 'bravura piece' which provides an opportunity for fine acting and splendid oratory in its starring role.

As one of the *Three Plays for Puritans*, *Caesar and Cleopatra* deliberately avoids both melodrama and erotic passion. Any hint of tragedy which might arise for example from comparisons with Shakespeare's dramatisation of the two main figures is quickly dispelled by comic anti-climax and absurdity. And although Shaw's Cleopatra is very feminine and preoccupied with romance, Caesar does not become infatuated with her. Their relationship is that of teacher and pupil: Caesar instructs Cleopatra in how to rule as a queen (similarly, in *Saint Joan*, Joan scolds and cajoles the childish Dauphin into behaving like a king). *Caesar and Cleopatra* doubly debunks the romantic heroism in its portrayal of Caesar. On the one hand, it shows him as a rather ordinary middle-aged man, who goes unrecognised by Cleopatra to begin with. Caesar pretends to no high moral code, is without illusions or sentimentality, and is notably sane and sensible, humble and humane. However, Shaw insists that despite his closeness to prosaic fact rather than heroic fantasy, Caesar is after all an extraordinary man with a genius for power. He is far more remarkable than any romantic hero. Like Joan, he has clearer vision than those around him, and is far ahead of his time. His leadership is exercised through his strong will, which is in harmony with the evolutionary purpose of the species. Because of this, Caesar has no need of conventional virtues such as generosity: Shaw writes of him, 'Having virtue, he has no need of goodness'. Despite its debunking of historical romance, *Caesar and Cleopatra* exploits spectacle for its dramatic effects, with many changes of setting, and exotic costume. Major historical events surround the action of the play, which itself focuses directly on small domestic incidents.

Shaw and Shakespeare's histories

Shaw's history plays, and in particular *Caesar and Cleopatra*, invite comparison with Shakespeare as well as with nineteenth-century historical dramas. The very title of *Caesar and Cleopatra* recalls Shakespeare's *Antony and Cleopatra*. Moreover, Shaw described *Julius Caesar* as a 'splendidly written political melodrama', and criticised Shakespeare's characterisation of Caesar as the 'travestying of a great man as a silly braggart'. For his own play he deliberately chose a different episode, much earlier in the sequence of events than the grand passion of Mark Antony and Cleopatra. He even emphasised the difference between his play and Shakespeare's by making Cleopatra refer in anticipation to her romance with Antony. Whereas Shakespeare shapes the story as tragedy, Shaw keeps it within the realm of comedy. *Saint Joan* also departs from its Shakespearean antecedent, and Shaw stressed in the Preface that his Joan was very different from the enemy witch of *Henry VI Part One* (and, he insisted, more historically accurate).

Shaw's rejection of the approach taken by Shakespeare is consistent with the noisy campaign which he conducted against him, denouncing Shakespeare's plays as splendid rhetoric and poetry without moral or philosophical substance. This stance was however ironically exaggerated, and adopted by Shaw in order to emphasise the distinctive and different character of his own play-writing. Later in his career he fully acknowledged the greatness of Shakespeare's achievement, and certainly his own plays show that Shaw knew Shakespeare very well and was considerably influenced by him. So the histories of Shaw and Shakespeare may be compared, as well as contrasted.

The chronicle play

In the Preface to *In Good King Charles's Golden Days* Shaw wrote: 'The "histories" of Shakespeare are chronicles dramatised; and my own chief historical plays, Caesar and Cleopatra and St. Joan, are fully documented chronicle plays of this type. Familiarity with them would get a student safely through examination papers on their periods.' *Saint Joan* is subtitled 'A Chronicle Play in Six Scenes and an Epilogue'. The subtitle suggests that Shaw modelled his play on the histories of Shakespeare, which used as their source material the historical narratives known as chronicles.

The term 'chronicle' is descriptive of the nature of Shaw's historical drama, as well as of its structure. The chronicle, an early form of history, comprised objective documentation of the chronological sequence of events, and was concerned with factual accuracy rather than with cause and effect or with interpretation. The Old English Chronicles, compiled partly under the direction of King Alfred the Great, remain the main source for the history of England between Bede and the Norman conquest. Shakespeare's histories and tragedies make substantial use of the sixteenth-century chronicles such as those of Holinshed. However, Shaw's claim that his histories, like those of Shakespeare, present fully documented objective facts is slightly misleading. In fact, Shakespeare's history plays do provide a moral and political interpretation of events. The plays focus individually on the themes of kingship and the evils of usurpation, and overall, the chronological sequence from *Richard II* to *Richard III* shows the restoring of order in the state in accordance with God's providential purpose. *Saint Joan*, even more explicitly, engages in debate as to the significance of events, and is concerned with historical ideas and forces. And Shaw cared rather less about meticulous research for his play than about his own understanding of the historical personages and events.

Another feature of the chronicle was the sequential and episodic nature of the historical narrative. This episodic structure is taken over into drama. In *Richard III*, for example, each scene is self-contained, and makes a particular point about Richard's moral deterioration, and the punitive effect of a guilty conscience. *Saint Joan* is divided into scenes which focus on distinctive episodes in Joan's story, and the play is structured in a simple, forward movement directly related to the chronological sequence of events, from the siege of Orléans, to Charles's coronation, then to the trial and execution of Joan, and finally to her rehabilitation and canonisation. The 'chronicle' effect of these dramatised episodes allows the play to work as a combination of moral exemplum and political debate. It links *Saint Joan* with the plays of Bertolt Brecht (1898–1956) as well as with Shakespeare's histories. Brecht's *Galileo* (1943) is an historical drama of the chronicle type. Both Shaw and Brecht wrote dramas of political ideas, concerned with the significance of human choice and action, and the interplay of historical forces.

Anachronism and Shaw's idea of history

Shaw castigates Shakespeare, in the Preface to *Saint Joan*, for writing about Joan from the viewpoint of the Renaissance. By contrast, he says, the medieval atmosphere blows freely through his own play. In fact Shaw freely employs anachronisms of style and ideas in *Saint Joan*, as in all his history plays. The colloquial speech of Joan is full of nineteenth- and twentieth-century idioms. The conversation in Scene IV between Warwick and Cauchon allows these characters to discuss Protestantism and Nationalism in a way which is not really within the compass of their fifteenth-century consciousness. Moreover, the arrival of the Gentleman in the Epilogue is a deliberate total anachronism of character and situation.

Anachronism in *Saint Joan* is a shock tactic, designed to prevent the audience from becoming immersed in the theatrical illusion of the past, and so detaching themselves from their contemporary reality. Shaw relies on the jarring incongruity of anachronism to startle the audience into a critical frame of mind. So the anachronisms are not merely a flippant or irresponsible disregard for authenticity. The lack of historical perspective is part of Shaw's idea of history. Like Brecht, he is concerned not with the past as different and remote from the present, but rather with analogy and repetition of events, issues and attitudes. Anachronism may help to highlight similarities with the past, and so keep the audience aware of the relevance of history to their own contemporary situation. The value of history for Shaw lies in its coherent interpretation of the past, which may appear as a predictor or determinant of the present and future. Subjective interpretation by the historian is not only inevitable but desirable, so that history will illuminate continuing issues such as justice, punishment and freedom, and help towards an understanding of social change.

The historical case of Joan and contemporary issues

Although the play is often anachronistic, Shaw nevertheless took care to dramatise the story of Joan in its historical and cultural contexts. In an article written for the New York Theatre Guild in 1924, he declared his interest in the 'great historical case of Joan of Arc', and stated that the 'real protagonists of the drama' were 'the Catholic Church, the Holy Empire, and the nascent Reformation'. So, in the play, Joan's historical case is represented as being intimately bound up with the issues of Protestantism, feudalism and nationalism in the Middle Ages, as well as more generally embodying the perennial conflict between the individual and repressive institutions. Shaw's interpretation may be challenged by historians, with respect, for example, to his analysis of emergent nationalism. However, it is useful to remember that in dealing with such topics Shaw is looking both backwards, to the Middle Ages, and around him, to the society of his own day. It is possible to identify a number of topics of contemporary relevance in *Saint Joan*.

Saint Joan and Irish nationalism

The theme of nationalism, which Cauchon expresses as 'France for the French, England for the English', may be related to twentieth-century Irish nationalism. The invasion and occupation of France by England during the Hundred Years' War suggests an analogy with the continuing conflict over political independence and autonomous government for Ireland. Sir Roger Casement, the Irish nationalist who was hanged as a traitor by the British in 1916, is mentioned in the Preface. Patrick Pearse and other Republican leaders were executed following the Easter Uprising of 1916. The Government of Ireland Act (1920) divided Ireland into two self-governing areas. The Parliament of Northern Ireland was opened in Belfast in 1921, and the following year the Irish Free State was established.

The topics of national identity and patriotism, and of territorial conflict, are also relevant to the First World War.

The Hundred Years' War and the First World War

The Hundred Years' War has a further analogy in recent history, with the First World War of 1914–18. This war was also known as the 'Great War', and 'the War to end all Wars', and it was felt, particularly

in 1916–17, that there was no way of ending it. Shaw saw Joan's canonisation as an expression of French nationalistic feeling in the after-
math of the war. The contemporary relevance of *Saint Joan* is supplied
partly by an implicit comparison of the fifteenth-century historical
situation with recent events in Europe. This too was a war fought over
territorial issues; indeed, the primary reason given for England's
declaration of war on Germany in 1914 was the latter's violation of
Belgian neutrality. England and France were allies in the First World
War, whereas they had fought each other in the Hundred Years' War.
This exchange of roles is a reminder of the arbitrary designation of a
national enemy, and so supports Shaw's satire against jingoistic
nationalism like that of the English Chaplain de Stogumber. The issue
of patriotism is also raised in *Saint Joan* by Warwick's deal with the
enemy to protect his own interests, and by the English soldier's 'unpatri-
otic'gesture in giving a cross to Joan.

An audience of 1923 or 1924 would have seen very clearly the relevance of Cauchon's prophecies of apocalyptic destruction in Scene IV.
He warns of 'blood, of fury, of devastation', and prophesies that 'The
world will perish in a welter of war'. To an extent, there is an ironical
reversal, in that the world has not perished; but the attitude that contemporary events showed the end of a cycle or epoch of civilisation and
the advent of a world 'wrecked back into barbarism', was fashionable
and widespread just before and after the First World War.

The military figures of *Saint Joan* help to establish the setting of
war. There are commanders, La Trémouille and La Hire, the professional soldier Dunois, the ordinary French soldiers about whom we
hear and who give Joan their support, and the rough English soldier.
The English soldier is the type of the ordinary anonymous private in
the trenches, good-humoured, sensible and unheroic. This figure
recalls the war poetry of Wilfred Owen (1893–1918), and also of Sieg-
fried Sassoon (1886–1967), who satirised the generals and bishops as
opposed to the ordinary fighting man. 'What do they all amount to,
these kings and captains and bishops and lawyers and such like?' says
the soldier in the Epilogue. 'They just leave you in a ditch to bleed to
death'. By contrast with this, we hear much of Joan's comradeship
with the French soldiers.

Feminism

Joan's own role as a female soldier recalls the mobilisation of women
in the First World War. During the war women worked at home as bus
drivers and in munitions factories, and at the front as nurses and
ambulance drivers. In the Preface Shaw mentions Edith Cavell, the
English nurse who was shot by the Germans in Belgium for sheltering

Allied soldiers, and who was celebrated for her pioneering work in nursing and for her patriotism. In Scene V, after the fighting is over, Joan wonders how she will cope with civilian life on her father's farm. After the war, women were expected to return to their domestic roles, relinquishing their new occupations to the men returning from battle. They thus lost some of the ground which had been gained for the cause of emancipation.

Joan is criticised by her judges for dressing as a man, and for preferring soldiering to traditional female occupations. This assertion of her individuality is seen as immoral, and as politically subversive: her unwomanly behaviour is a protest against the male hierarchy. Feminist revolt became a political force in the early twentieth century, when the suffragist movement fought for women's rights. The Women's Social and Political Union, founded by Mrs Emmeline Pankhurst in 1903, campaigned in London from 1906 against Liberal parliamentary candidates. From July 1912 the WSPU adopted more militant tactics, including arson. Suffragettes, including Mrs Pankhurst and her daughter Sylvia, were imprisoned; some were forcibly fed when on hunger-strike. When war broke out militant action was suspended. However, women were not given the vote on the same terms as men until 1928.

Sylvia Pankhurst is mentioned briefly in the Preface to *Saint Joan*. Later, in a radio talk broadcast in 1931 on the five-hundredth anniversary of the burning of Joan of Arc, Shaw directly compared Joan to Sylvia Pankhurst. Both women found 'the whole power of society marshalled against them' in their crusade, and both suffered torture for their beliefs.

Shaw's use of historical material

Shaw's immediate source of historical material for *Saint Joan* was T. Douglas Murray's account of the trial, entitled *Jeanne d'Arc Maid of Orleans, Deliverer of France: Being the Story of Her Life, Her Achievements and Her Death, as Attested on Oath and Set Forth in the Original Documents* (1902). This was a full translation of Quicherat's transcription of the trial of 1431 and the rehabilitation proceedings of 1456. Shaw had seen a production of the play by the American Percy Mackaye, *Jeanne d'Arc* (1906), which was based on Murray's account. He regarded Mackay's portrayal of Joan as too sentimental and pathetic. It is likely that he was also familiar with Tom Taylor's *Jeanne Darc (Called the Maid); a Chronicle Play, in Five Acts* (1871). The two plays show a close resemblance of structure and incident, which may be attributed to their use of the same source material. In writing *Saint Joan*, Shaw also had in mind versions of Joan's story by Voltaire,

Schiller, Mark Twain, Andrew Lang and Anatole France. However, he was concerned less to emulate those writers than to produce his own personal and, as he thought, more accurate account. Shaw's distinctive interpretation of the historical facts is evident in the play, as for example, in the sympathetic portrayal of Joan's judges. Similarly, Shaw draws attention to his individual dramatic shaping of the story by alluding to the conventions of different kinds of drama such as historical romance and romantic tragedy. The rapturous acclaim which ends Scenes II and III is suggestive of heroic or romantic historical drama. In Scene II the Archbishop's sigh undercuts this mood, and the heroic expectations of Scene III are reversed by the following scene. The play also alludes to representations of Joan as a romantic heroine, only to reject these as inappropriate and inaccurate.

Shaw modified the historical material in adapting it for the stage. He wrote of Joan's trial that it was 'a drama ready made, only needing to be brought within theatrical limits of time and space to be a thrilling play'. The trial scene of *Saint Joan* compresses events of several months in 1431 into a single episode. Shaw applied this method of dramatic compression to the entire story. The first scene conflates the historical Joan's two visits to Vaucouleurs, in 1428 and 1429. The events on which Scene II is based cover the time from Joan's arrival at Chinon in February 1429 to the Dauphin's provision of troops in April of that year. The Archbishop's initial reluctance to admit her to the court is a representation of the extensive examination by ecclesiastical authorities to which Joan was submitted on the Dauphin's orders. In this way Shaw re-shaped the evidence to create dramatic interest. As might be expected, such modification also applies to the historical figures. For the purposes of dramatic characterisation Shaw often needed to expand and fill out the evidence. One example is the Inquisitor Lemaître, to whom Shaw attributes great skill and intelligence. He also uses Warwick as spokesman for the feudal system.

Joan as a heroine

Shaw satirised the values of historical romance, yet his own history plays take as their central characters famous historical figures: Caesar, Napoleon, Joan of Arc. He did in fact regard the hero as a positive force, and his view of history recognised extraordinary individuals as incarnating the historical process. However, as a playwright he was adamant in working to eliminate the stereotyped heroes, heroines and villains of melodrama, as wholly untrue to the conditions of real life. This attitude is not inconsistent, although it may seem so. Shaw identified the dramatic convention of stage melodrama with conventional morality, which he regarded as outworn and over-simplified. He also rejected the concept of the romantic hero as falsely idealistic, with an artificial code of honour. But although he rejected the heroes and villains of romance and melodrama, Shaw substituted his own brand of hero, either historical or fictitious. The Shavian hero is a prosaic realist, like Napoleon, or Bluntschli in *Arms and the Man* (1894), whom Shaw contrasts with the romantic hero Sergius Saranoff. The hero is also a vitalist, struggling for change against a system which is inherently conservative. Shaw's historical plays explore the problem of the interaction, or clash, between the vital hero and the artificial system.

Dunois in *Saint Joan* has some of the characteristics of the romantic hero, but he is fundamentally realistic. He learns from Joan to renounce the feudal art of war in favour of pragmatic fighting tactics. The Dauphin has some of the features of Shaw's realists. Joan herself is a female version of the Shavian realist and vitalist, and one in a long line of unconventional and determined girl heroines.

Aristocracy and feudalism

The concept of the romantic hero is associated with the aristocratic tradition, which Shaw attacked in a number of plays including *Arms and the Man*. During the nineteenth century there was a tendency to idealise the aristocratic order of the Middle Ages. However, Shaw depicts the feudal aristocracy in *Saint Joan* as artificial, effete and corrupt. The members of the Dauphin's court, such as Gilles de Rais and the Duchess de la Trémouille, are polished and elegant, but also proud, snobbish and rather silly. The court itself is in disarray, seething with petty squabbles, rudeness and rivalry. Charles has no real power, and is always in debt. The barons despise him as weak and unreliable. Shaw is not merely satirising aristocratic behaviour and privilege; there is a suggestion, in the unsatisfactory relationship between Charles and his feudal lords, that feudalism is no longer an effective system of political and economic organisation.

The cunning and corrupt Earl of Warwick is the spokesman in the play for the feudal aristocracy. He fears a threat to feudalism in Joan's support for the Dauphin. The logical outcome would be a dismantling of the feudal order, its replacement by a political and economic unit centring on the king and the nation. This would mean less power for the feudal lords. As the Church is the equivalent of the feudal system in the religious sphere, both barons and bishops would stand to lose their authority by such a change: hence the deal which is struck by Warwick and Bishop Cauchon.

Against the feudal aristocracy, Shaw sets the bourgeois and democratic spirit as represented by Joan.

Joan as a saint

The title of *Saint Joan* (in particular the use of the word 'Saint' in full instead of the more usual abbreviation 'St') draws attention to its selected focus. Shaw's designation of Joan as 'Saint' confirms his estimate of her, yet at the same time the play invites a reconsideration of what it means to be a saint.

On the one hand, Shaw's portrayal of Joan strips sainthood of supernatural and orthodox religious connotations. Although Joan is obviously extremely religious (indeed, the Archbishop says she is infatuated with religion) she is not excessively virtuous or pious. She is seen praying just once, briefly, at the opening of Scene V. Her voices and visions are crucial to her, but she takes them as a matter of course. They are not discussed extensively, and play no significant role in the action. Joan does not indulge in spiritual meditation or self-mortification, and has no longing for martyrdom. Even her 'miracles' are questionably supernatural, and rather trivial. Moreover, the miraculous aspect of sainthood is undermined by the Archbishop's natural explanation, by Charles's vulgar attitude (he recalls in Scene II the tricks of levitation performed by his grandfather's personal saint), and by the credulity and superstition of the other characters. Overall, *Saint Joan* demystifies, desupernaturalises and secularises sainthood.

Yet, on the other hand, the claim of sainthood which the title makes is a serious one. The canonisation in 1921 of Joan of Arc as a Saint of the Catholic Church provided the occasion for Shaw's play, which is concerned with the role of the saint in society. The Epilogue shows Joan's canonisation as retrospective recognition of an individual whom the contemporary political and ecclesiastical systems could not tolerate. But as well as considering the public and official aspects of sainthood, the play also shows Joan as a saint in herself, although of a peculiar Shavian kind.

The saint and vital genius

Joan is a saint of Shaw's secular religion of creative evolution. She is a vital genius who incarnates the evolutionary appetite, *élan vital* or life force which can be equated, in Christian terms, with the will of God. Her creative vitality is evident in her energy and enthusiasm, and her driving sense of purpose. Shaw's vital heroines include Ann Whitefield in *Man and Superman*, Lina in *Misalliance*, and perhaps Eliza in *Pygmalion*. Joan can be compared with Major Barbara, and with Lavinia in *Androcles and the Lion*, in terms of her creative vitality and intensity of faith. Her visionary qualities recall those of the clairvoyante Mrs George in *Getting Married*, and her extraordinary powers those of the

Ancients in *Back to Methuselah*. The Ancients were a race of superior beings, far advanced in evolutionary terms, whose mental and physical powers transcended material limitations. Although Joan is not a supernatural saint in the orthodox sense, there is after all something of the miraculous and the mystical about her.

Reaction to the Shavian saint

Saint Joan was favourably received by both Catholics and non-Catholics, but the play was by no means wholly uncontroversial as a religious drama. Catholic feeling was sensitive to Shaw's balanced account of Joan's trial and his sympathetic portrait of the Inquisitor Lemaître. Catholic Action's condemnation of Shaw's view as incompatible with the official position of the Church was largely responsible for the failure of the project to film *Saint Joan*. Earlier, in 1925, the Rationalist J. M. Robertson published *Mr Shaw and 'The Maid'*, a full-length book which attacked the historicity of *Saint Joan*. Reviewing this book for the *Criterion* in 1926, T. S. Eliot (a convert to Anglo-Catholicism) also denounced Shaw's play, as a superstitious effigy erected to Joan. Atheists and materialists could object to the miraculous and the mystical in Shaw's saint, believers to the way in which the supernatural was discredited.

Joan and Christ

The play establishes an analogy between the story of Joan and that of Christ. There are persistent references to the Gospel narrative, and direct verbal echoes. In Scene II, for example, Joan asks the Dauphin, 'Wilt be a poor little Judas, and betray me and Him that sent me?' Here and elsewhere her speeches suggest a parallel with Christ. De Stogumber also compares himself with Judas, and after Joan's execution he comments, 'Some of the people laughed at her. They would have laughed at Christ.' Joan's isolated position before hostile assessors in Scene VI recalls Christ, brought before Pilate. And in some ways her defiance of the medieval Church is similar to Christ's challenge to the orthodoxy of Judaism. Moreover the shape of the play recalls the narrative of Christ's Passion, Resurrection and Ascension, as it was dramatised in the medieval pageant-drama of the mystery cycles. The Epilogue is the equivalent of the appearance of Jesus to His disciples following the Resurrection, and His Ascension and transfiguration. Finally, the parallel between Joan and Christ is reinforced by imagery and symbolism. For example, the kingfisher which in Scene III is indirectly associated with Joan, is a traditional symbol of Christ (as in the poetry of Gerard Manley Hopkins (1844–89)).

The analogy drawn between Joan and Christ works in two ways. On the one hand, Shaw uses it to emphasise that Joan is not only a saint, but a messianic figure. On the other, the boldness of the comparison underlies the near-blasphemy and megalomania of Joan's claim to direct divine inspiration.

Structure and dramatic method

In thinking about dramatic structure, it is helpful to separate out the historical events which form the basis of the story from the way in which Shaw has chosen to shape his play. We might say that Scenes I–VI are built around three main historical events: the siege of Orléans (Scenes I–III); the coronation of Charles VII (Scene V); the trial and execution of Joan of Arc (Scene VI). The Epilogue is built around two subsequent events: the rehabilitation of Joan in 1456, and her canonisation in 1920. But this historical framework does not in itself tell us very much about the *dramatic* shaping of *Saint Joan*, nor about the function of individual scenes. We might go on to say that the play falls into two main parts, followed by an epilogue. The first part (Scenes I–III) shows Joan's rise to success; the second part (Scenes IV–VI) shows her downfall. The epilogue restores her to glory. This breakdown tells us a little more about the dramatic structure, and indicates something of Shaw's dramatic purpose. According to this division Scene IV marks the turning point of the action, at the end of the first part. Joan has fulfilled one of her stated objectives, in raising the siege; Scene IV marks a pause before the second stage of her mission, the coronation in Rheims Cathedral. Yet it is notable that Joan does not appear at all in Scene IV. What is the function of this scene? How else might Shaw have chosen to dramatise this part of the story? We might expect, from the build-up of excitement in the first three scenes, that he would show us, immediately following on, the triumph of the French at their success. Instead, the scene is set in the English camp, quite some time after the siege. This shift in location and time tells us something about the function of the scene. Its effect is

(a) to prevent us from being totally involved with Joan, as the heroine of a success story;
(b) to direct our attention towards the significance of Joan's actions, and the forces at work around her.

So Scene IV introduces the plot against Joan, and prepares for the darkening mood of the play. The discussion between Warwick and Cauchon suggests various interpretations of her, as Protestant or Nationalist. Notice that de Stogumber's function is to provide a kind of commentary on their sophisticated ideas from the point of view of the average man. At this point in the play, then, the dramatic emphasis moves away from action towards discussion. In Scene V Joan discusses her position with the Court, and in Scene VI the trial is also a lengthy debate as to her innocence or guilt. To sum up, Scene IV marks a turning point in that

(a) the play subsequently deals with Joan's downfall;
(b) the mood darkens gradually;
(c) action gives way to discussion, and a generalising of Joan's case to consider broader issues and ideas.

Could anything be added to this list?

Another way of looking at the structure is to observe, instead of a sequence of historical events, a sequence of locations. The setting moves from the rural castle in Scene I, to the court in Scene II, to the army camp in Scene III and thence to the enemy camp, Rheims Cathedral and so on. Each is a carefully chosen location which signifies a particular context in which Joan can be placed, and each contributes to the overall picture of her role in society. Moreover, the settings of court and castle are of a particular kind, and suggest an analogy with fairy-tale or pantomime (in fact, there are resemblances to the situation, dialogue and characters of pantomime in Scene I; and the Epilogue resembles the 'transformation scene' in which all ends happily after the dark times of Scenes IV–VI). The fairy-tale motif of the princess in disguise is here replaced by the saint in disguise. In Scene II, La Hire says that Joan is 'an angel dressed as a soldier'. In a literal or a figurative sense Joan wears a number of disguises: country girl, soldier, angel, witch, heretic. The movement of the play might be described as a gradual penetration of her disguise to discover the true Joan. In Scene VI she is apparently revealed as really a heretic, but this too turns out to be a disguise. The Epilogue finally reveals her as a saint. To look at the play in this way is not to suggest that the story of Joan is fundamentally a fairy-tale, but to detect the dramatic methods which Shaw uses, in order to see what conventions he is setting the story *against*. The fairy-tale or pantomime quality of the dramatic structure underlines by contrast or incongruity the seriousness of Joan's story. The motif of disguise links up with the theme of the recognition of Joan as a saint; it is an example of how Shaw uses dramatic methods and conventions to support the themes of his play.

Recognition scenes

The recognition scene is just such a convention, which is found in various kinds of drama, from Greek tragedy to melodrama. One example of a recognition scene in *Saint Joan* is the episode in Scene III where Joan identifies the Dauphin. Other examples involve recognition by particular characters of Joan's mysterious powers and inspiring qualities. At the end of Scene I Robert de Baudricourt exclaims 'She did come from God.' Do we accept this as a genuine recognition? It follows on immediately from the comic miracle of the hens laying. What in Scene I leads us to agree or disagree with de Baudricourt? It would be useful to think of as many recognition scenes as possible in the play, and describe their function and effect.

Overall, *Saint Joan* might be thought of as a recognition play, leading towards the climax of the recognition that Joan is a saint, which is implicit in her canonisation. Another term for recognition is 'discovery'. Do you find this concept helpful?

Conversion scenes

In Scene I Robert de Baudricourt is converted to the belief that Joan is divinely inspired, and persuaded to send her to Chinon. This is the first conversion which Joan makes within the play itself, although we have already heard of the way she has converted the soldiers, and Bertrand de Poulengey reports his own conversion. Each of the first three scenes of the play hinges on characters being converted to Joan's cause, in a sequence of ascending importance. Which characters are converted in Scene II? Are they all equally convinced of Joan's divine mission? Which matters more in producing these conversions, Joan's 'miracles' or her character? The conversion scenes demonstrate Joan's ability to persuade and inspire others, and to create belief. They indicate a vital aspect of her rise to success. Correspondingly, in the second part of the play, it is her reduced credibility which contributes to her downfall. In Scenes I–III, the factors involved in conversion – an alleged miracle, Joan's arguments, her charismatic personality, political considerations – are carefully delineated, and we are invited to assess Joan and her converts accordingly. The conversion of Chaplain de Stogumber provides structural continuity in the second part of the play. In Scene IV he believes Joan to be a witch and a heretic, and says that he would burn her with his own hands. By the end of Scene VI he is converted by actually seeing her burnt; this conversion points forward to the Epilogue, which will reverse the verdict of the trial and so condemn the execution.

As was the case with recognition scenes, conversion scenes are an example of the way in which the craft of the play, its dramatic methods and devices, matches the themes which concern Shaw. You might like to go beyond this to consider to what extent the play as a whole is a strategy to convert the audience to a particular view.

Dramatic expectation

Scene I introduces Joan, and Scene II the Dauphin: in each case we hear a good deal about the character before she or he appears, and certain expectations are set up for us. In Scene II the attitudes expressed by the Dauphin's courtiers indicate that there are problems at the court and in the country generally. After the Dauphin enters, it is clear that things cannot go on as they are: so we anticipate, before Joan enters (and having already seen her for ourselves), that her intervention will produce some change. A warning note of expectation is sounded later in the scene, when the Archbishop prophesies danger in Joan's love of religion. This setting up of a dramatic expectation is similar, although on a larger scale, to the test of Joan engineered by Charles and Bluebeard. In fact the entire play is constructed around a pattern of expectation and fulfilment, both within individual scenes and from scene to scene.

So, at the end of Scene I, de Baudricourt orders Joan to go to Chinon. It is expected that she will encounter some difficulty in being admitted to the Dauphin's presence: the early part of Scene II confirms that expectation. The main part of the scene focuses on her recognition of the Dauphin, and then on her reception by the court. The expectation which carries forward from the end of Scene II is Joan's command of the army at Orléans, and her meeting with Dunois, dealt with in Scene III. Scene IV sets up the expectation of the plot against Joan, and Scene V fulfils the earlier expectation of her coronation of Charles. It is fair to say that in the first part of the play, the expectation is that of success; in the second part, we no longer look to successive scenes for success, but for eventual failure, and a tragic outcome. Overall, Shaw's use of dramatic expectation provides for continuity and connection between the separate episodes. Particularly in the first part, it provides a rapid rhythm and forward movement, constantly throwing us forward to future events in a simple progression. However, the effect is not merely that of dramatic suspense: the audience is invited by the pattern of expectation and fulfilment to give a verdict on what happens, and to assess the play's interpretation of events.

The historical basis of the play sets up certain expectations in itself. The outcome is already decided, and an informed audience will know it in advance. All historical plays share this feature: does it lessen dramatic suspense, or alter it in some way? The emphasis is thrown onto *how* and *why* events occur, onto cause and effect, significance and implications. You should distinguish between the external expectations which arise from historical facts, and the way in which Shaw uses expectation as an internal dramatic device. Notice how the pattern of expectation and fulfilment is signalled in the dialogue. In Scene II, for example, when the test of recognition has been arranged, La Trémouille exclaims, 'I wonder will she pick him out', and the Archbishop predicts how she will succeed in doing so. Shaw often draws attention to the question of what is to happen, and how, by the device of allowing the characters to voice their expectations. Can you find other examples?

Ironic reversal

However, what happens in the play is often not the fulfilment of our expectation, but the reverse of what is expected. The pattern is one of expectation followed by ironic reversal. Several such reversals may be found within a single scene, providing a structural framework for the scene. Within Scene VI, for example, major reversals occur at the points of Joan's recantation, and then again at her relapse; but there are other, minor reversals as well. What is the function of such reversals? As well as introducing an element of surprise, they may lead us to reconsider our expectations, and assess whether what has happened is not after all more appropriate. In Scene VI, the reversals emphasise the debate as to whether Joan is innocent or guilty of heresy, and how she is to be punished. Again, an involvement in this debate is signalled by the dialogue, as when de Stogumber asks, 'do you mean that you are going to allow this woman to escape us?'

A pattern of ironic reversal underpins the overall dramatic structure. *Saint Joan* moves through two reversals in Joan's status: from being acclaimed as saviour in Scenes I–III, she is denounced as a heretic in Scene VI, and then again declared a saint in the Epilogue. The verdict of heresy is reversed by rehabilitation and canonisation. The final ironic reversal occurs at the prospect of the saint's return to earth: she would be denounced once more.

Shaw's use of dramatic expectation and reversal is related to his challenging of conventional values. Joan's unconventional style of behaviour and dress may shock the audience as well as the characters in the play, especially as this departs from what they expect of a saint.

Saint Joan as tragedy

In the Preface Shaw subdivides *Saint Joan* into the romance of Joan's rise, the tragedy of her execution, and 'the comedy of the attempts of posterity to make amends for that execution'. This subdivision corresponds to Scenes I–III, Scenes IV–VI, and the Epilogue respectively. Scenes I–III combine historical romance and fairy-tale. Shaw's use of the term comedy to describe the Epilogue is partly structural, meaning that it ends happily. The Epilogue and the first two scenes are also comic in situation and tone: the mood darkens into tragedy from Scene IV onwards. We have already seen that the shaping of the play follows the rise and fall of the heroine: this is a traditional tragic pattern, which embodies a concept of tragedy as a sudden and catastrophic reversal of fortune.

In Scene V the Archbishop tells Joan 'you have stained yourself with the sin of pride. The old Greek tragedy is rising among us. It is the chastisement of hubris'. The Archbishop, who is a man of classical learning, has in mind the concept of tragedy as it appears in ancient Greek drama, where the downfall of the hero is the inevitable outcome of an overweening pride and ambition which offend the gods. The Archbishop's denunciation of Joan's pride may be supported by Shaw's claim in the Preface that his play is classical, even Aristotelian, tragedy (as defined by Aristotle in his famous treatise, the *Poetics*).

A number of factors might be considered in deciding whether *Saint Joan* is a tragedy, and if so, of what kind. Does the play depict Joan's pride as a sin or a tragic error, or rather as the natural expression of vital genius? Is what happens to her punishment for sin, or simply the outcome of a tragic but inevitable conflict between the individual and society? A feature which *Saint Joan* shares with classical and Renaissance tragedy is that the heroine's actions and sufferings are bound up with the fate of the community. And is the play, considered as a whole, tragic in its effect? Some audiences and critics have considered that the tragedy of *Saint Joan* is weakened and spoilt by the comedy of the epilogue. Joan's tragedy is confined to the historical moment of her execution: from the perspective of the twentieth century this tragedy is reversed. By dramatising this reversal, Shaw cancels out the tragedy. However, other critics maintain that the play *is* finally tragic, and *because* of the Epilogue rather than *in spite* of it. They suggest that an optimistic idea of progressive evolution is countered by the implication that the entire process would be repeated if Joan were to return to earth. This represents a tragedy for society and mankind: the tragic conflict is not only inevitable but irreconcilable and eternal. This view goes against Shaw's statement that the Epilogue is a comedy. Which view do you agree with?

The Epilogue

In the Epilogue the mood of the play changes from tragedy to comedy. There is also an abrupt shift of dramatic method, away from theatrical realism, which is heralded by the appearance of Joan's spirit. The Epilogue has a dreamlike quality, but is not consistent even as Charles's dream. Later in the scene the entry of the Gentleman from 1920 again disrupts the illusion; it strikes even the other characters as incongruous.

The non-realistic dramatic method of the Epilogue foreshadow's

Shaw's later extravaganzas. His political extravaganzas include *The Apple Cart, On The Rocks* and *Geneva; Too True to be Good* and *The Simpleton of the Unexpected Isles* are philosophical extravaganzas. The extravaganza is a comedy of ideas, which combines fantastic settings and action with discussion and debate. The plot and characterisation are minimal: Shaw simply assembles a group of representative figures, and allows each to speak for a particular point of view. The method of the extravaganza can be traced back to Shaw's earlier plays, such as *Back to Methuselah* and *Misalliance*. It has a dramatic antecedent in nineteenth-century burlesque, including the satirical operettas of W. S. Gilbert (1836–1911). Shaw's extravaganzas can also be compared with expressionistic drama of the twentieth century.

The extravaganza form allows Shaw to exploit and subvert further the conventions and expectations of bourgeois realism, and therefore also to challenge conventional values. Elements of incongruity, surprise and discontinuity accordingly make a positive contribution to the meaning and effect of the play. The treatment of Joan's canonisation in the Epilogue oscillates between farcical irreverence and rhapsodic praise. The ending is anti-climactic and thought-provoking, and Joan's final question is left unanswered. Perhaps the earth will be ready to receive saints like Joan when it has reached a more advanced stage of moral evolution. On the other hand, perhaps such saints will never be tolerated, because the conflict between conservatism and mediocrity on the one side, and original genuis on the other, will never be resolved. The Epilogue does not deliver a final verdict. Shaw wishes the audience to go on thinking about the issues which have been raised.

The characters of *Saint Joan*

The main characters of *Saint Joan* are all based on historical figures. However, Shaw elaborated on the historical material, creating dramatis personae appropriate to the kind of play he wished to write. On the whole (with the possible exception of Joan herself) his purpose in drawing these characters was not so much to explore in depth their individual psychology and motivation, but rather to dramatise them as embodying attitudes or voicing issues which he presented as being implicit in, or suggested by, the historical situation of the play. *Saint Joan* depicts in its characters a range of types and attitudes, such as the cynical Archbishop, and the bigoted and superstitious Chaplain de Stogumber, the shrewd, political Earl of Warwick, and so on.

This range creates dramatic interest, and most of the characters are highly individualised. It also demonstrates various attitudes which may be adopted towards Joan. Indeed, many of the characters are dramatised largely in terms of how they respond to her. Accordingly, the attention of the audience is focused on the variety of possible interpretations and assessments of the figure of Joan, and the historical events of her trial, execution and canonisation.

Joan

Joan is the central figure of the play; indeed, the entire action is built around her. She is portrayed as a heroine, saint and martyr, but of a rather unusual kind which may not fulfil our expectations. For example, she is down-to-earth rather than romantic or pious, and she seeks to avoid martyrdom by confessing that she is a heretic. Perhaps in order to emphasise Joan's untypical qualities, Shaw shows other characters as being constantly surprised and shocked by what she says and does. Nevertheless, Joan is an extremely attractive figure, who invites liking and admiration. She is clearly very different from the other characters, and often appears far more sensible as well as courageous. However, Shaw makes us realise how easily Joan's personality and behaviour could provoke and infuriate, although our attitude towards her is sympathetic. You may notice that although Joan is the central figure, Shaw does not permit her any extended reflection or analysis of her situation. She is presented as a woman of action, and we learn little of her private thoughts and feelings.

It is clear from the start, when Joan first enters to demand horses and soldiers, that she is realistic and practical, with no romantic illusions. She is dedicated to her mission, and determined to get what she wants. Joan's view of life is simple and straightforward. She has complete confidence that she is right, and acts on the assumption that other people will see things her way and cooperate with her. In fact, de Baudricourt and later the Dauphin and Dunois are overwhelmed by her energy, directness and enthusiasm. Joan's forceful manner is combined with persuasive charm and good humour. She has an innocent faith in the goodwill of others. Her simplicity and directness are reflected in her frank colloquial speech. Shaw makes her speak in dialect, to emphasise the bluntness of a country girl and a soldier, unaffected by the artificial politeness of the court. Joan's manner of address to de Baudricourt and the Dauphin also shows that she is not daunted by authority or social rank, although she does display great reverence towards the Archbishop. Joan is strikingly independent in her opinions and behaviour. She rejects the conventional role and dress of a woman, is totally uninterested in marriage, motherhood or romantic involvement, and longs simply to be a soldier and mix on equal terms with men. As for her private voices and visions, she thinks these are nobody's business but her own. On religious matters, she defers to Church authority only as long as it does not conflict with her own judgment.

Joan's leadership depends on her personal magnetism, and her capacity to inspire others, especially the Dauphin and Dunois, with her own energy and enthusiasm. But her enthusiasm is always backed by common sense and sound reasoning, as when she listens to Dunois's military advice at the siege of Orléans. Even the orders which come from her saints agree with her own opinion of the need for the English to return to their country. Joan finds her courage in the excitement of battle, although she does not seek glory for its own sake: life without battles is dull to her.

In the first three scenes there are hints of the conception of Joan as the victorious heroine, the Maid of Orléans as depicted in romantic versions of her story. Successive episodes show her gathering yet more followers and achievements. However, even at this stage the Archbishop sees in her excesses potential danger and failure. In Scene V, after the Dauphin has been crowned, we see her unable to cope with the political situation at the court and in the Church. Her single-minded determination now appears as a complete refusal to compromise, or to understand or accept the views of others when they conflict with her own. So she may seem stubborn, proud, inflexible and even nearsighted in her understanding of the situation. She is unable to act politically, or adapt to changing circumstances. When the nobles withdraw their support she looks for the acclaim of the ordinary people. Similarly, at her trial she is ready to blame her judges and even her saints rather than herself. Joan's independence and unconventionality, and her insistence of her rightness, have left her totally isolated. Her reaction is not to accept advice or help, but to turn to her voices or, when these seem to fail her, to God. She does not deliberately seek martyrdom or self-destruction; indeed, she is intent on survival and escape, and will even confess to being a heretic if this will save her life. Joan's longing for freedom and independence make her imprisonment appear as the ultimate violence against the individual, worse even than death.

Joan's spontaneity and energy wane in Scenes V and VI, and she becomes depressed. She is wiser as to the complicated and corrupt ways of the court, but she still sees the situation in terms of a simple drama of support and persecution, with those who oppose her inevitably in the wrong. She sees herself as the heroine, and her understanding of her own role and behaviour is basically unchanged. In the Epilogue she recovers her liveliness and good humour, and displays a more sophisticated awareness, a degree of tolerance for the ideas of the other characters who can no longer affect or control her.

Charles

The Dauphin, later Charles VII, might be called the anti-hero of the play, or perhaps its clown figure. Certainly the incongruity of his playing the role of a ruler is apparent in his first entry. He is aware of his own shortcomings in comparison with his royal predecessors, and has no wish to assume the responsibilities of kingship. He cannot command the respect of his nobles, to whom he is constantly in debt. Moreover, he is a coward, and fears fighting. He would rather lead a quiet life and settle matters by a treaty. He behaves like a naughty and spiteful child, whose sulks and cheekiness enrage La Trémouille and earn him a scolding from the Archbishop. He is bullied and ridiculed by the court, and regarded as a weak, stupid and ineffectual ruler. He seizes eagerly on the chance to have his own personal saint and champion in Joan, to protect him against the others.

In actuality, however, Charles is not at all stupid. He is shrewd and realistic, and capable of acting with pragmatic self-interest. For example, his desire to negotiate a settlement rather than fight is not mere cowardice but a preference for common sense over foolish heroic gestures. Moreover he holds his own against the nobles, and succeeds in having his own way. Inspired by Joan's courage, he assumes full authority as king. Whereas other characters are dead or discredited by the end of the play, we see from the Epilogue that Charles has survived, and gained more power. He has even become a more positive leader, engaging directly in battle. Shaw depicts in Charles the reverse of conventional romantic ideas of a hero, king and leader. He has no heroic pretensions, and takes the world as it is. He is the realist, whom Shaw prefers to the alternative of the more glamorous hero with romantic ideals. The weak, unimpressive coward nevertheless succeeds.

Despite the developments in his status and power in the course of the play, Charles remains petulant and self-centred. He shows no gratitude to Joan after the coronation, and even resents her success and popularity. He seems to have a callous disregard for what is to happen to her, and does nothing to save her from capture and execution. Nevertheless, Charles understands Joan far better than most of the other characters do, and appreciates her strength and greatness. In the Epilogue, he also perceptively predicts that she would be rejected if she returned to the world. He and Joan like and respect each other. If Charles were a romantic hero, he might be Joan's fairy-tale prince. We might expect their friendship to develop into a romantic involvement; although in the Epilogue Joan laughs off this remote possibility as unrealistic.

As well as individualising Charles's personality, Shaw suggests in his relationship with the court that some of his ineptitude as a ruler can be attributed to the political situation. Charles is a feudal king without any real power over his barons and lords, and with no real wealth to call on. The clashes at court, between his petulance and their bullying, stem from an unsatisfactory and deteriorating economic and political system. Shaw depicts a crisis of feudalism as well as the crisis for the authority of the Church represented by Protestantism.

Dunois

Jack Dunois, the Bastard of Orléans, has the enviable reputation, according to Bluebeard, of being a brave and invincible warrior and a handsome, irresistible lover. He is the closest the play gets to a full-blown romantic hero. However, his heroism is closer to that of Shaw's realists, and rests on practical good sense. Dunois is capable and good-natured, without affection or romantic illusions. He is caught up by Joan's enthusiasm for battle, and when the wind changes direction he is convinced that her mission is from God. However, he is aware of her limitations as well as her powers, and acts as her mentor in military strategy. Joan listens to his advice, and in turn Dunois learns from her ideas, renouncing the medieval art of war with its conventions and ritual in favour of pragmatic use of men and weapons. Dunois quickly becomes fond of Joan, and she of him. Shaw hints at a romantic relationship between them, as the play's hero and heroine. When Joan talks to Dunois about love, marriage and children, this alerts us to the possibility of their marrying. However, the possibility is not a real one, and their intimacy is not sexual or romantic. It is a professional comradeship, based on equality and shared interests. Dunois genuinely supports Joan, although he has misgivings about her overconfidence and foolhardiness. He does not make any heroic attempts to save her. He himself survives, to prove his ability as commander of the Dauphin's army. We learn in the Epilogue that he has succeeded in driving the English out of France.

Warwick

The Earl of Warwick, commander of the English army in France, is a sophisticated and worldly nobleman, with the confidence and pride of wealth and high social rank. In the play he is the representative of feudal aristocracy. He prides himself on his broad experience and enlightened outlook, and is not narrowly bigoted or patriotic. Indeed, he is not committed to any faith or cause, and his main interest is not in victory for England, but in the continued stability of the feudal order. To him Joan's call for increased power for the king represents a threat to the position of the feudal lords, and he determines to destroy her. Warwick is a shrewd, cunning and unscrupulous politician and diplomat. He negotiates a deal with the Bishop of Beauvais whereby he will deliver Joan up for trial by the Church, and subsequently have her put to death. When Joan has been captured, Warwick is impatient for the

1 12

trial to be concluded. He makes sure of her death by a show of force, and a hasty, improperly conducted execution. Warwick has no personal hatred for Joan, but regards her death as a political necessity. Similarly, his dealings with Cauchon are a matter of expediency. He cares nothing for Joan's religious claims, and in the Epilogue smoothly congratulates her on her rehabilitation. Warwick embodies the machinations of corrupt power, without moral principle. In this character Shaw draws on the traditional villain of melodrama.

Cauchon

Peter Cauchon, Bishop of Beauvais, a dignified and powerful churchman, is steadfast in his devotion to the Church, whose authority he regards as above that of king or state. He insists on the Church's right to proceed against Joan without taking account of political considerations. He genuinely and passionately believes that Joan's heresy, like those of Wycliffe and Hus, represents an insidious and growing threat to the Church, and to the whole of the civilised world. Although he does not share Warwick's estimate of Joan, and dislikes his political motives, he is prepared to strike a deal with him in order to bring the heretic to justice. His aim, however, is to procure Joan's salvation and, if possible, to save her life as well.

Before the trial Cauchon warns Warwick against political interference. His dedication to justice and to the Church is clear, and he is revolted by Warwick's cynicism and unscrupulous methods. In the court, he delivers a vehement warning, pointing to the ruin which Joan's heresy could bring. His emotional commitment is such that he cannot keep complete control of the court, and he reacts violently to the interruptions of the Chaplain and Courcelles. However, he is concerned that the trial should be just and proper: he dismisses the Chaplain's call for Joan to be tortured, and is impatient of any diversion from the main charge of heresy. He insists on pronouncing solemn excommunication before Joan is removed from the court, and is shocked at the impropriety of her hasty execution.

In the Epilogue we learn that Cauchon has subsequently been discredited, in the process of Joan's rehabilitation. He deplores this unjust treatment, as he acted in good faith and according to his duty. Moreover, he sees in this pronouncement of history an omen of danger to the Church. At the end, he acknowledges the value of Joan's assertion of the direct relationship of the individual with God; but he would still condemn her as a heretic if she returned to earth. Shaw depicts Cauchon as a just man, caught up in the urgency of the issues but acting with integrity as well as intense moral conviction. This characterisation enables the figure of Cauchon to represent the Church's case against

Joan, and counters the expectation of him as a villain set up by other accounts of Joan's trial.

The Inquisitor

The Inquisitor, Brother John Lemaître, is intelligent, shrewd, and subtle. He judges the correct moment to intervene in the proceedings of the Bishop's court, and assume responsibility for Joan's trial. Unlike Bishop Cauchon he is able to maintain a cool detachment in handling the court, and dealing with objections and interruptions. His gentle and persuasive manner helps him to deal with people. The Inquisitor is a masterly rhetorician and a clever lawyer, and is learned in the law of the Church. He is deeply committed to the aims of the Inquisition, and defends its role as necessary, just and even merciful. He gravely denounces heresy as inspired by the devil, and warns of its deceptive simple and humble origins. He believes that heresy must be rigorously pursued and eliminated, and argues that the apparent harshness of the Inquisition may actually save the heretic from mob violence. Although the Inquisitor's long speech is carefully argued and apparently reasonable, its denunciation of heresy rests principally on a fear, which is perhaps irrational and exaggerated, that heretics inevitably encourage sexual perversion.

The Inquisitor is careful to ensure that the trial is conducted properly according to the law, although he is ready to help Joan if she will recant. He is less horrified than Cauchon at her hasty execution, seeing the point of order as a loophole which might be useful later in a reassessment of the case. We find, moreover, that the Inquisitor after all believes Joan to be innocent of any evil design, although technically guilty of heresy. Her simplicity and ignorance have unwittingly earned her excommunication, according to the system of Church law which he represents. However, the Inquisitor's clear-sightedness should not be confused with cynicism. He acts with integrity and a sense of duty.

Shaw allows the Inquisitor to put the case for the Inquisition as cogently as possible. Moreover he ironically gives this representative of a harsh if not cruel judiciary system a mild, even kindly temperament. In doing so he may have modelled his character on the historical Torquemada, a notorious figure of the Spanish Inquisition. The force of this characterisation is to prevent the audience from arriving at an easy condemnation of the Inquisitor as the villain of the story. Shaw's Inquisitor cannot be written off as a medieval torturer; indeed, his arguments against heresy and in support of repression may be compared to much more recent justifications of extreme punitive measures taken against crimes held to be subversive to society. In this way Shaw's characterisation of Lemaître works against an oversimplified interpretation of Joan as the innocent victim of a cruel system, and a comfortable discussion of the historical past as remote and irrelevant. However, his portrayal is not a vindication or adequate defence of the Inquisition; rather it exposes and explains the attitudes towards law and punishment which sustain such a system.

The Archbishop

The Archbishop of Rheims is intelligent, sceptical and sophisticated. He is a rationalist who scorns superstition, and holds that miracles are not supernatural phenomena but natural occurrences which by coincidence or contrivance inspire faith. He is dismissive of reports of Joan's miraculous powers, and attempts to prevent her admission to the court. He is however quick to recognise her powers of leadership and inspiration, although he does not join in the ecstatic acclaim. He is obviously touched by the reverence with which Joan greets him, perhaps because he is isolated and treated disrespectfully by the courtiers. Nevertheless he sees in Joan's piety a dangerous infatuation with religion. In Scene V, after Charles' coronation, he warns Joan that her pride will lead to a tragic downfall, and that she will reject the advice and protection of court and Church at her peril. For all his unorthodox ideas, he stands by the dignity and authority of his office, and condemns Joan's defiance of the Church.

Shaw has drawn the Archbishop as a complex and interesting figure. He represents the order of the medieval Church, yet is at the same time alienated from contemporary attitudes. He foreshadows a new, rational spirit of enquiry, closer to the Renaissance, with its humanism and return to classical learning, than to the Middle Ages. Indeed, he is aware of historical forces at work, and senses the coming period of change.

de Stogumber

Chaplain John de Stogumber is an unintelligent and bigoted English churchman. He is irrational, impetuous and given to emotional outbursts. He thinks and acts according to simple moral categories of good and evil, and regards Joan as a witch and a heretic. In his ardent patriotism and blind devotion to the Church he hates and fears her as the arch-enemy of both England and Christianity. He trusts to the Inquisition to punish Joan without mercy, and is eager for her to be put to death. The Chaplain is not, however, a cruel man, although he has something of the bully and the coward in his personality. He lacks imagination, and cannot anticipate the reality of suffering. When he sees Joan burnt at the stake, he goes to the other extreme of hysteria and despair, overwhelmed by guilt. The experience shakes him to the core. When we see him in the Epilogue he is a changed man, a gentle, weak-minded old person. Although he has been converted to the belief that Joan is a saint, significantly he does not recognise her spirit, just as he failed to recognise her innocence while she was alive. In this character Shaw depicts the common man, and suggests the destructive force of prejudice, ignorance, incomprehension and superstition which may harm an extraordinary individual such as Joan. There is also a hint, in the Chaplain's attitude to the conflict between England and France, of the jingoistic war fervour which Shaw had condemned during the First World War.

Martin Ladvenu

The Dominican Monk Martin Ladvenu is drawn as a complementary opposite to the English Chaplain. In contrast to de Stogumber, he is thoughtful, gentle and patient, and actively seeks to save Joan from the punishment of the court. He is liberal, tolerant and idealistic, and understands the issues involved in Joan's trial as a heretic. He sees Joan's errors as stemming from simplicity, rather than wickedness. He also believes implicitly in the methods and objectives of the Inquisition, and cannot suspect any political motives or compromise. However, in his own way, he like de Stogumber completely misunderstands Joan. He is shocked at her relapse, and cannot understand her reaction to the prospect of imprisonment. His grave composure after the burning contrasts with the hysteria of the Chaplain. After Joan's death he remains loyal to her cause, and regards her rehabilitation as the triumph of truth and justice. In the Epilogue we find him whole-heartedly committed to Joan, and shocked at the Dauphin's matter-of-fact response. In this character Shaw shows that the processes of the Inquisition can operate with the purest of motives.

de Baudricourt

Captain Robert de Baudricourt is apparently a strong-minded, decisive man who stands no nonsense. However, his vigorous and blustering manner hides a lack of will-power, and he is easily influenced by others. His resolve not to grant Joan's request is undermined by the persuasion of Joan herself and of Poulengey. De Baudricourt sends her to the Dauphin, but still worries about whether he has made the right decision. His reaction to the apparent miracle of the hens laying shows him to be superstitious and credulous. However, the Captain does at least recognise that Joan's ability to inspire courage will be of assistance in the campaign.

Minor characters

Bertrand de Poulengey is thoughtful, decisive and resolute, despite his absent-minded and slow habit of speech. He is prepared to back his conviction that Joan might save the military situation, by paying for her horse.

Monseigneur de la Trémouille, commander of the Dauphin's forces, is quick-tempered and something of a bully. He is rude to the Dauphin, whom he despises. He is neither educated nor very intelligent, and does not understand the Archbishop's explanation of miracles. He is furious when Charles gives Joan charge of the Army.

Gilles de Rais, known as Bluebeard, is a smart, self-possessed young courtier. He likes to impress others with his elegance and wit, although his gaiety is a little forced. It is he who poses as the Dauphin in order to play a trick on Joan. Joan regards him as an idle fellow, and reproves him for his impudence to the Archbishop.

Captain La Hire is a typical soldier, rough-spoken and superstitious, but good-humoured. He finds Joan's eloquence and determination irresistible, and is one of her most loyal followers.

The *Steward* to de Baudricourt is downtrodden and obsequious, and quails before his master's anger. He is extremely superstitious.

Canon John D'Estivet, the Promoter of the ecclesiastical court, is by no means open-minded or sympathetic towards Joan. He questions her sharply, pounces eagerly on any evidence of heresy, and is quick to call for her excommunication.

Canon de Courcelles, one of the Bishop's assessors in the Church court, is unintelligent and superstitious. He believes Joan to exert a diabolical influence over the court. He makes noisy and foolish objections to the proceedings, but is intimidated by the Inquisition and the Bishop. He is bewildered and discouraged by the response to his demands, and does not comprehend the issues of the trial, or discriminate between trivial and serious changes. It is he who calls for Joan to be tortured.

We hear about the *English Soldier* at the end of Scene VI, although he does not appear until the Epilogue. He is rough and plain-spoken, but his good deed in making a cross for Joan, reported by the Chaplain, shows common humanity and natural mercy. He has little sympathy or fellow-feeling for those in authority. He is a representative of the common man, and may suggest the ordinary, anonymous soldier of the Great War.

The *Gentleman*, a twentieth-century Church official who announces Joan's canonisation in the Epilogue, is formal and correct, and lacking in a sense of humour.

Of the three Pages, *Dunois's Page* is the most individualised. He is a lively, forthright boy, whose quick eye catches sight of the kingfisher and the change in the wind's direction. He joins eagerly in shouting support for Joan. *Warwick's Page* addresses his master in a pert and irreverent manner, and is undaunted by the authority of the Church dignitaries. The *Court Page* is given a slight distinguishing feature in his peremptory calls for silence before he announces arrivals at the court.

The *Duchess de la Trémouille* is a very small speaking part in Scene II. She is proud and disdainful of Joan, and magnificently dressed.

Style and character

Shaw is often thought of as the master of dazzling witticisms and pointed repartee. However, the dialogue of *Saint Joan* is generally written in a plain, direct prose, which ranges from the colloquial to the more formal, and is well suited to intelligent discussion. Nevertheless, there is a good deal of variation, and Shaw adapts the style to the character who is speaking. Individual touches are given to characters through idiosyncratic vocabulary, idiom, and syntax or sentence pattern. Some of these distinctive features may be related to the occupation or class, as well as the personality of the speaker. So, Captain La Hire, for example, speaks with the rough diction of a soldier, and uses characteristic oaths. The speech of the churchmen tends to be more elegant and formal: the Archbishop's style is polished and urbane, with an undertone of irony.

Bishop Cauchon first speaks to Warwick in Scene IV in a measured, careful way. However, as the scene develops he uses a vehement and impassioned rhetoric, and sounds as if he were actually making a speech. This is particularly true of his long oration on heresy. The emotional and poetic intensity of his style is indicative of the strength of his feelings on the subject of heresy. His speech is full of figurative language: metaphor, describing heresy as a 'pestilence', and as 'cancerous'; simile (Mahomet 'ravaged his way west like a wild beast'); and vivid images of blood and destruction. Another striking simile is found in the Epilogue, where he says that 'The solid earth sways like the treacherous sea'. His tendency towards grand generalisations is illuminated by the following passage from Scene IV:

> It will be a world of blood, of fury, of devastation, of each man striving for his own hand: in the end a world wrecked back into barbarism.

The Inquisitor's careful, discriminating style shows a concern for precision in language, as well as in thought and judgment. Near the beginning of Scene VI he says: 'I must admit that this seems to be one of the gravest cases of heresy within my experience.' Notice the number of phrases here which qualify the underlaying statement that Joan is a heretic: 'I must admit', 'this seems to be', 'one of the gravest', 'within my experience'. The denunciation of heresy, later in the scene, is the longest formal set speech of the play: it combines the qualities of a sermon and a lawyer's address to a court. The Inquisitor is skilled in rhetoric, and his address makes full use of devices such as repetition, antithesis and parallelism. It gives an impression of reasonableness and logic, with its informative and reassuring tone, and the carefully chosen factual details which support the argument. Not surprisingly, Cauchon comments: 'I do not see how any sane man could disagree with you.'

Joan's speech is on the whole plain and direct. Her short, clipped sentences in Scene I suggest a practical and down-to-earth personality. Shaw makes her use a form of dialect at certain points in the play, with non-standard syntax and pronunciation: for example, 'Coom' instead of 'Come', 'Be you captain' instead of 'Are you the captain'. She also addresses the Dauphin with the now archaic 'Thou'. This is not an accurate transcription of any specific regional dialect: Shaw uses it loosely to suggest Joan's provincial origin, her class, and her easy, unaffected manner. But Joan's speech can also be rhetorical and lyrical, as in Scene V when she talks to Dunois about the voices she hears in the bells. Joan becomes even more rhapsodic at the end of Scene VI, in the final long speech which follows her recantation. This speech has a biblical ring, reminiscent of the cadences of the Authorised Version: 'Bread has no sorrow for me, and water no affliction'. Its cumulative rhetorical patterning, using balance and repetition, builds towards the emotional climax of 'the blessed, blessed church bells'. Joan's rhapsodic style is always associated with her accounts of her visionary experiences, and is deliberately heightened above the level normally tolerated even for dramatic dialogue. In fact at both extremes of dialect and rhapsody Shaw emphasises or singles out for attention Joan's style of speaking, to mark her off as different from all the other characters.

Charles's chatty, conversational style is not at all formal or elevated – perhaps not what we might expect from a king. Most of what he says centres on his own experience and feelings, and indeed many of his sentences begin with 'I'. He is given to sarcastic retorts, as when he says to the Archbishop 'Thank you. You are always ready with a lecture, aren't you?'; or later, 'I will read it for you if you like. I can read, you know'. His staccato style, with short speeches and sentences, sounds irritable and petulant, but also suggests a quick, nervy intelligence. Unlike other characters, he does not use smooth, polished rhetoric to disguise his feelings.

Warwick is fluent, well-mannered, and adept at polite speech, as when he greets Cauchon with 'My dear Bishop, how good of you to come'. Shaw marks him out as a nobleman by making him speak in the conversational style of modern upper-class English. Dunois's attempts at poetry at the beginning of Scene III introduce the imagery of the west wind, and set the lyrical tone of the scene. However, the awkwardness of the attempt marks this style as out of character for the straightforward, plain-spoken commander, and Dunois soon reverts to a less elevated speech.

Language and situation

The dialogue does not only vary according to which character is speaking. Additionally, the dramatic language is adapted to the situation, and to the topic of a speech. Bishop Cauchon, for example, expresses himself in emotional rhetoric when he talks about heresy. Joan's dialect is most pronounced at the start of her conversations with the Dauphin in Scene II and the Epilogue, and when she first meets Dunois. The effect is to emphasise the incongruity of the country girl addressing the king or the knight. Joan's rhapsodic style when she talks about the bells and her voices actually embarrasses the other characters. In this case Shaw adapts her language not to suit the situation, but to jar with it.

Most of the variations in style tend, however, towards appropriate usage in a given context (what is termed in linguistics the 'register' of a particular language situation). The Inquisitor's address to the court combines the registers of the ecclesiastical and legal professions. Other specific usages in Scene VI include the pronouncement of excommunication, and the sentencing of Joan. This formal prose is very different from ordinary speech: its dramatic effect is to suppress the individual personality of the speaker and stress his official function. The recantation which Ladvenu reads out is an official document, using written rather than spoken language. It strikes us as not Joan's style at all, and so highlights the falsity of her position at this point. It is an example of language which is appropriate to the situation, but which does not fit the character: significantly, it is said *for* Joan, rather than *by* her. Shaw uses a similar device in the Epilogue, when the Gentleman reads out the formal proclamation of the 'claim of the said Joan of Arc to be canonised as a saint'. Joan interrupts, 'But I never made any such claim': her misunderstanding stems from a difference of usage, and emphasises the gaps between the public and the personal.

The language of the Epilogue differentiates markedly the various characters. Ladvenu's declamatory style has strong echoes of the Old Testament, in contrast to Charles's plain speech. The soldier sings nonsense verse. The Gentleman reads out an official document, and even when he speaks for himself he uses the style of a business letter: 'I have been requested by the temporal authorities of France to mention that . . . '. The contrastive use of language in the Epilogue goes beyond the specific dramatic situation or character delineation, to draw attention to language itself: the way it communicates meaning and even the way in which it shapes or constructs reality. The climax of the Epilogue is the litany of praise to Joan, which unites the characters in a single language act. In such liturgical language style actually becomes meaning: in this case, the recital is a ritual act of reverence.

The Epilogue displays most clearly an emphasis on language; but the play as a whole combines the styles of different situations – ecclesiastical, legal, courtly, official, colloquial. This variety of language and style may be compared with the variety of ways in which Joan herself is presented, as soldier, heretic and saint: it may express and reflect the relativity of meaning and truth.

Part 4

Hints for Study

Studying the play

Studying a play, especially for an examination, is in a sense an artificial exercise: you need to remember that *Saint Joan* was intended primarily for performance in the theatre, to entertain an audience. There are certain difficulties involved in reading a play, as opposed to seeing it performed: these difficulties may be alleviated if you try to visualise how the play might be staged and what response the dramatic action might elicit. Try, for example, to determine at what points the audience might be expected to laugh, and why. Pick out any especially theatrical moments, such as Joan's recognition of the Dauphin in Scene II, or the moment in Scene VI when she tears up her recantation, and consider how Shaw exploits the theatre here and to what purpose. Think what effect the ending of each scene might have, and what the audience might expect to see in the following scene. In this way you will be able to consider how *Saint Joan* works as a play, and how it is put together for actors and audience. This will tell you a good deal about Shaw's stagecraft, his use of dramatic conventions, and his purpose in writing the play.

The detailed stage directions and descriptions of character which Shaw included in the published text may help you in this process of visualisation. You may however think that some of them are more appropriate to a novel than to a play. Are there any directions which it would be difficult in practice for an actor to communicate to an audience? Can you find any which contain information that definitely could not be gleaned by the audience from the dialogue itself? What is the purpose and value of these descriptions?

When you are studying the play, pay attention to plot and structure, characterisation, themes and style. It is essential that you have a good grasp of the plot and the details of the dramatic action. Notice carefully what happens in each scene, and identify its climax and turning point. Decide how each follows on from the previous scene both as a distinct dramatic episode, and as one of a cumulative sequence. In thinking about the structure, notice any parallels or contrasts of character or situation, and any repeated motifs, as well as characteristic dramatic devices such as discovery or reversal.

Practice writing about individual characters, using various kinds of evidence: description of the character in the italicised stage directions; what other characters say about him or her; what the character says about himself or herself; what he or she says on particular topics. Does the character change in the course of the play? It is sometimes asserted that Shaw cannot create characters who are convincingly human, but that he simply uses them to voice certain ideas. In thinking whether or not you agree with this, you will need to examine your assumptions as to what a dramatic character is, as well as considering the characters of *Saint Joan*.

You will find a variety of themes in the play, ranging from nationalism or imprisonment, to women's role or the freedom of the individual within society, as Shaw develops the implications and contemporary relevance of the story of Joan. Try to assess the stance of the play in relation to these various topics, being careful to bear in mind the irony and balance of Shaw's treatment. Do not assume too readily that any one character is Shaw's spokesman: even if a character speaks with great eloquence and authority, this does not necessarily mean that Shaw sympathises wholly with his point of view. Beware too of relying on any single speech or passage to 'prove' Shaw's position. You should consider each character or statement in its context, and determine the stance and dramatic meaning by looking at the play as an intricate and complex whole.

Answering questions on the play

Criticism of drama, as of literature generally, involves communicating your interpretation and evaluation of the play, and is therefore necessarily subjective. It follows that there is no single 'correct' answer to any question: nevertheless, your essay must be based on a sound, well-informed argument, supported by illustration from the play. A thorough knowledge of the text is essential; this can only be achieved by careful re-reading and close study.

Before answering a question, think about its implications, and decide what evidence it calls for. Select and arrange your material, making rough notes if you wish. Your essay should contain several substantial points – say four or five – each taking up one or two paragraphs. Each point should be illustrated by detailed reference to the play, or by direct quotation. If you are asked to agree or disagree with a particular assertion about the play, you may organise your essay by giving alternative points of view in turn, and then by way of conclusion stating which you find more acceptable. Above all, keep your reader in mind: how much information do you need to supply? Will your reader understand what point you are making? Even an informed reader such as an examiner will expect you to demonstrate your knowledge of the play, but without tediously telling the story. You can achieve this by referring to the dramatic action, rather than paraphrasing the plot (unless, of course, you are specifically asked for a paraphrase or précis). Remind yourself from time to time of the question which you are answering, and check that each paragraph is relevant.

Be specific: it is a good idea when writing about a play to direct your argument towards individual scenes or parts of a scene. This will help you to focus on dramatic methods and themes, rather than writing loosely about the story of the play.

Illustrative quotations

You may illustrate your argument by detailed reference to particular passages, or by paraphrasing the dialogue; it may however be more succinct and specific to introduce quotations when you can. Select quotations carefully, and make sure they are relevant. Do not drop in a quotation without comment: it should be clear to your reader why you are using it. In general, beware of using too many or too long quotations.

It is a good idea to practise selecting quotations. As an exercise, find *three* quotations to illustrate each of the following, and decide how you would use them:

(a) Joan's attitude towards the authority of the Church
(b) the role of women in society
(c) the dangers of heresy
(d) the Dauphin's attitude towards being a king
(e) examples of superstition and prejudice in the characters
(f) the character of Warwick.

If you have learnt quotations for an examination, remember that they may not after all be relevant to the questions you are asked. Do not use a quotation simply because you have learnt it: irrelevant quotation will waste time and use up valuable space in your essay, and is unlikely to earn you any credit.

Evidence from outside the play

Your understanding and appreciation of *Saint Joan* may be greatly enhanced by biographical information about Shaw's life, ideas and interests. His professed atheism is clearly relevant, as is his interest in judicial systems and imprisonment. You will also benefit from an awareness of the social, historical and cultural context in which the play was written and first performed. The character of the soldier takes on a particular quality when you recall that the First World War had recently ended. You may also find it helpful to consider the play in the light of Shaw's Preface, and of his other non-dramatic writings. A knowledge of Shaw's other plays may lead you to recognise themes and patterns, and to identify a characteristic Shavian style and method.

However, such evidence should be used sparingly and with great care when it comes to answering questions on the play. Bring in this information only when it is relevant to a specific question and illuminates something in the play. The main focus of your essay should be the play itself.

Historical information

Similarly, historical information about the life and martyrdom of Joan of Arc, and the Hundred Years' War between England and France, is very useful. You should, however, be careful to distinguish the plot from the historical facts: notice which incidents Shaw has chosen to dramatise, and how he has shaped the historical material. The historical background to Scenes I–III is the siege of Orléans, but we would not say that these scenes are primarily about the siege. The siege, as well as the coronation of Charles, and the burning of Joan at the stake, are all important and well-documented historical events; but Shaw presents them obliquely, and the events take place off-stage. Is this solely because of the difficulties of staging such incidents? What aspects of the story has Shaw chosen to highlight instead? Unlike Joan's execution, her trial is dramatised very fully: this shows where Shaw's interest lies. At the centre of the play, in Scene IV, he places the discussion between Warwick and Cauchon, which is an extrapolation from historical fact. Notice that this discussion ranges over the historical implications and broader issues arising from Joan's case. Again, this tells us a good deal about Shaw's use of historical material and his conception of the play.

If you use historical information in an essay, make sure that what you have said contributes to the argument. Remember that *Saint Joan* is a play, not an historical document, and that you are writing about it *as* a play.

Review questions

1. Describe briefly the historical drama of the nineteenth century.
2. Discuss Shaw's use of the historical background in *Saint Joan*.
3. Find *four* examples of anachronism in *Saint Joan* and discuss their dramatic function.
4. What features does Joan share with a conventional romantic heroine, and in what ways is she different?
5. In what ways is social class depicted in *Saint Joan*?

6. Discuss the position of women in society as depicted in the play.
7. Discuss the theme of nationalism in *Saint Joan*.
8. Examine the representation of miracles in the play.
9. In what ways does Shaw present Joan as a saint?
10. Say briefly what you understand by dramatic reversal, and discuss *two* examples from the play.
11. Find *two* examples of recognition scenes, and discuss their dramatic effect.
12. What is the effect of Shaw's use of dialect and colloquialism in the play?
13. Write a brief account of each of the characters in *Saint Joan*.
14. Show how style and dialogue contribute to characterisation in the play.

Detailed study questions

The following questions are designed to help you in your revision of the play:

Preface
1. What view does Shaw take in the Preface concerning Joan's voices and visions?
2. What parallels does Shaw draw between the trial and execution of Joan, and the operation of systems of justice in twentieth-century society?

Scene I
1. What do you learn about Joan from the conversations between Robert de Baudricourt and his Steward, and Robert and Bertrand de Poulengey?
2. What impression of Joan have you gained from her behaviour and speech in this scene? What arguments does she put to de Baudricourt?
3. Why does Robert de Baudricourt decide to send Joan to the Dauphin?

Scene II
1. Why is Monseigneur de la Trémouille angry?
2. Describe the relationship between Charles and the court.
3. Why does the Archbishop not wish Joan to be admitted to see the Dauphin? What makes him change his mind?
4. Does the Archbishop believe in miracles? What if any 'miracles' does Joan perform in this scene?
5. What does Joan's recognition of the Dauphin tell us about her?
6. Why does Joan say that Charles should fight? Why does Charles not wish to be crowned king?

7. Write an account of the scene between Joan and Charles, saying what effect Joan has on the Dauphin.
8. Why does the Archbishop give Joan his blessing with a sigh?

Scene III
1. What is the function of the page in this scene?
2. Why does Dunois long for a west wind?
3. Compare your impression of Dunois in this scene with what Blue-beard said about him in Scene II.
4. What military advice does Dunois give to Joan?
5. What persuades Dunois to join forces with Joan and accept her command?

Scene IV
1. Would you describe the effect of the transition from Scene III to Scene IV as one of anti-climax?
2. What does Warwick wish to discuss with Bishop Cauchon?
3. What stage has the conflict between England and France reached?
4. Why does Bishop Cauchon think Joan is a heretic rather than a witch? What in his opinion should be done with Joan?
5. What danger does Warwick consider Joan to present to the feudal aristocracy? What fate does he wish for her?
6. What does Warwick mean by calling Joan a Protestant? What does Cauchon mean by calling her heresy Nationalism?
7. What impression have you gained of the Chaplain from this scene? What does he think of Joan? Why does he wish her to be burnt to death?
8. What agreement do Warwick and Cauchon reach about Joan?

Scene V
1. Why is Joan discontented at the beginning of this scene?
2. How does Charles react to his coronation? Is his reaction what you would have expected?
3. Account for the response of the various characters to Joan's announcement that she intends to return to her father's farm.
4. Compare the views of warfare expressed by Joan and Dunois. Why does Dunois think that Joan is likely to be captured?
5. How does Joan's 'pride' manifest itself in this scene?
6. Find two points of disagreement between Joan and the other characters. Whose viewpoint do you sympathise with?

Scene VI
1. What stage has Joan's trial reached? Why does the Inquisitor intervene in the proceedings of the Bishop's court?
2. What are the main charges brought against Joan? Write a brief account of the argument and evidence used in each case, and say

whether or not you find Joan's answer to the charge convincing.
3. Write a précis of the Inquisitor's speech on heresy.
4. Why does Joan agree to sign a recantation? Why does she relapse into heresy?
5. What is irregular about Joan's execution? Why does the Inquisitor not intervene to stop it?
6. Summarise the proceedings of the trial. Say whether you find the trial and verdict fair.
7. What is Martin Ladvenu's attitude towards Joan? Compare the behaviour of Ladvenu and de Stogumber after the execution.

Epilogue
1. Is the Epilogue Charles's dream?
2. Why is Charles pleased at the result of the inquiry?
3. Describe the relationship of Charles and Joan in this scene. Has Joan changed?
4. Who gives the more convincing self-justification, Cauchon or Warwick?
5. Why is the Soldier described as a saint?
6. Discuss the dramatic function of the Gentleman.
7. Briefly account for the disappearance of each of the characters. Why is the Soldier the last to leave?
8. Attempt to provide an answer to Joan's final questions and consider their implications as an ending to the play.

Sample answers

1. Discuss the significance of the title of *Saint Joan*.

Shaw's choice of title for *Saint Joan* reflects some of the similarities and differences between his dramatisation of the story of Joan, and other versions with titles such as *The Maid of France, Die Jungfrau von Orleans*, and *Jeanne Darc*. Like these other versions, *Saint Joan* concentrates on the historical figure of Joan of Arc. However, Shaw's Joan is not a stereotyped romantic heroine, with idealised qualities and virtues. He emphasises her practical good sense, her forthright manner, and her strong will. She is not conventionally feminine; moreover, any hint of romantic interest in the plot is firmly dismissed.

The feature indicated in the title, which distinguishes the play from other, earlier versions, is that Joan is a saint. Shaw's use of the full form 'Saint', rather than the abbreviated form 'St' draws attention to this. Joan had been canonised by the Catholic Church in 1920, only three years before the play was written. As the title suggests, the play focuses on Joan's status as a saint, and on the historical process leading to her canonisation. She was condemned as a heretic in 1431 but in 1456 the sentence was revoked and the trial declared corrupt. *Saint Joan* does not restrict its focus to Joan's life and personality, or to events of the fifteenth century. It shows Joan in relation to the Church and the Court, and examines the political and religious forces which determined her execution as a heretic. The Epilogue reaches as far as Joan's recent canonisation. The play's themes include the role of the saint in society, and such broader issues as the conflict between a radical individual and repressive conservative systems, or between freedom and social order.

Joan is presented as a saint, although of a rather unusual kind. The play does emphasise her faith in her voices and visions, her devotion to the Church (when its orders do not go against her judgment), and her dedication to her divine mission. Several miracles are credited to her supernatural powers, as when the hens start to lay again in Scene I, or the wind changes to the west in Scene III. However, these so-called miracles are all capable of rational or natural explanation, and overall Shaw takes care to ensure that it is unnecessary to account for Joan's sainthood in supernatural terms. Moreover, Joan is not excessively virtuous, or inclined to spiritual meditation. She does not long to be a martyr: her recantation in Scene VI is made with the wish to save her life.

So Shaw does not depict Joan as a saint in the conventional sense, but from a more secular aspect, equating sainthood with natural genius. In the Preface he compares her as a genius with Newton and Socrates, and suggests that she was also a bearer of the life force or evolutionary appetite. Creative evolution is not explicitly referred to in the play itself; but Joan is characterised as vital, strong and determined. She is a gifted individual, a natural leader with vision and ability beyond the ordinary. However, those same qualities also lead to conflict. It is the problem of the genius, saint or rebel in society, which leads to the paradox and irony in the Epilogue of the simultaneous acclaim of Joan as a saint, and rejection of her proposal to return to earth.

Although the play endorses Joan's recognition as a saint, it does not condemn out of hand her original trial or her judges. The longest scene of the play is a full dramatisation of her trial whereas the rehabilitation and canonisation are only reported, in the Epilogue. Shaw presents a balanced view of the Bishop and the Inquisitor, who conduct the trial with professionalism and integrity. Just as Joan is not sentimentalised or idealised as a heroine or saint, so there are no villains among her judges.

The title is thus appropriate to the themes and structure of *Saint Joan*. It gives a good indication of what the audience is to expect, even though the play itself fulfils those expectations in a way which may challenge conventional attitudes.

2. Compare and contrast the Chaplain John de Stogumber and Brother Martin Ladvenu.

John de Stogumber is described as a '*bullnecked English chaplain of 50*'. He is stupid, hot-headed and bigoted in his opinions, blindly patriotic and extremely superstitious. In Scene IV his comments provide a foil to the sophisticated debate between Warwick and Cauchon, who he admits are 'too learned and subtle for a poor clerk like myself'. He attributes the defeat of the English to Joan's witchcraft, and is eager for her to be burnt at the stake. At Joan's trial, in Scene VI, he makes emotional outbursts, protesting vehemently at the reduction of the charges against her. He is unable to understand the difference between trivial allegations and the serious issue of heresy. His hatred and fear of Joan stem from ignorance, and he is devastated by witnessing the reality of her burning. In the Chaplain Shaw presents a satirically exaggerated portrait of the jingoistic 'John Bull' figure of the average Englishman.

Brother Martin Ladvenu is a French Dominican monk who acts as one of Joan's assessors. He is younger than de Stogumber, and described as ascetic in appearance. Unlike the Chaplain he is intelligent, scholarly and patient. He treats Joan with gentle consideration throughout the trial scene, and believes that the Inquisition should proceed mercifully, with the aim of saving Joan's soul and if possible her life. When she recants he says 'Now God be praised that He has saved you at the eleventh hour'; whereas de Stogumber asks in alarm, 'do you mean that you are going to allow this woman to escape us?' Ladvenu is a far more sympathetic character than de Stogumber; however, although he pities Joan's innocence and simplicity, he does not really understand her, and is shocked at her relapse. In the character of Ladvenu Shaw shows that even a gentle, merciful and intelligent man can be implicated in the cruel processes of the Inquisition. Ladvenu believes implicitly in the Church and in the Inquisition.

The Chaplain and Ladvenu are drawn as contrastive characters, and Shaw invites us to consider them in relation to each other. This is particularly clear at the end of Scene VI, when each in turn reacts to Joan's execution. Ladvenu's grave composure is in marked contrast to the Chaplain's hysterical guilt and despair. However, there is another ground for comparing the two characters at this point in the play, in that both are now converted to a belief that Joan came from God. There are other similarities between them. Both are patriotic: even Ladvenu fervently hopes that it was the English who laughed at Joan. Both are devoted to the Church. More importantly, they are ordinary men with a simple view of good and evil: they have no awareness of any political motives operating in Joan's case.

In the Epilogue the two characters again appear separately. Ladvenu, fanatically committed to Joan's cause, speaks in an evangelical manner. The Chaplain, now a senile country priest, has been permanently affected by his experience. However, he is still blind to Joan's qualities, and does not recognise her spirit.

---

3. How far can *Saint Joan* be described as a comedy?

The first two scenes of *Saint Joan* contain many comic incidents and situations. The opening, in which Squire Robert de Baudricourt scolds his cringing Steward, is close to knockabout farce; the incident of the hens which refuse to lay is reminiscent of the broad comedy of pantomime. In Scene II there is comedy of disguise and (potentially) mistaken identity, when Bluebeard plays a trick on Joan by pretending to be the Dauphin. In both scenes there are comic reversals, arising for example from the shocking effect of Joan's unconventional speech, behaviour and dress.

Comic characters include de Baudricourt, Captain La Hire and the Dauphin. De Baudricourt's thundering anger and his decisiveness both appear foolish. La Hire's resolve not to swear is repeatedly and comically broken. The Dauphin's appearance and behaviour are unfitting for a king, and he is the butt of the courtiers' ridicule. However, we laugh with the Dauphin as well as at him, because of his sly wit and sarcastic observations. Even in the later stages of the play he seems more like the court jester than the king. In Scene V Shaw uses him to inject a note of comedy, when he complains about the weight of the coronation robes and the rancid holy oil. The English Chaplain is ridiculed as stupid and superstitious: however, since such stupidity and prejudice can cause harm, there is a serious edge to the satire.

Comic language in the play ranges from witticism to colloquial abuse. Joan's bluff and direct speech often makes other characters appear ridiculous: her reference to 'old Gruff-and-Grum' raises a laugh at La Trémouille's expense. Pretentiousness is often deflated by comic retort, as when Joan asks 'Be that Queen?', and Charles replies 'No. She thinks she is'.

The Epilogue is a comedy of ideas in the form of an extravaganza. The Soldier's description of Hell is a comic inversion of the conventional concept of hell. The entry of the Gentleman provides incongruity of situation and character, in the form of comic anachronism. The Epilogue can also be described as comic in the structural sense, in that Joan's 'resurrection' and canonisation are a happy ending. Shaw described the Epilogue in the Preface as 'the comedy of the attempts of posterity to make amends' for Joan's execution. The absurdity of the reversal involved in declaring her a saint is suggested in the officious dignity of the Gentleman, whose dry, formal manner appears funny to the other characters.

The Epilogue has been criticised as being too flippant, and as being a comic anti-climax which spoils the drama of the previous scene (although it is also possible to see the ending as deeply tragic, leaving Joan once more rejected, and completely alone). Up to this point the mood of the play has darkened steadily. However, the comic anti-climax and jarring incongruity are a deliberate device, designed to reawaken in the audience the critical spirit which belongs to comedy. Moreover, we may note that Shaw regarded comedy as a fundamentally serious dramatic form, even more profound perhaps than tragedy.

Saint Joan draws on many different types of comedy, and its mood changes rapidly and frequently even within a single scene. The movement of the play towards a darker emotional tone is not straightforward, and its comedy is not confined to the opening scenes. Comedy is found even in the scene of Joan's trial: for example, in the absurd charges which the Chaplain and Courcelles wish to be brought against her, and in de Stogumber's sulky refusal either to sit down, or to stand, at the Inquisitor's request.

Some further questions

1. Is *Saint Joan* a tragedy?
2. Discuss the contribution made by the Epilogue to the play.
3. Discuss *Saint Joan* as a religious drama.
4. Find examples of imagery and symbolism in the play, and consider their function and effectiveness.
5. In the Preface Shaw writes of Joan: 'There were only two opinions about her. One was that she was miraculous; the other that she was unbearable.' How far is this an over-simplification of her character as it appears in the play?
6. Write brief accounts of the following dramatic incidents, and say how far, and in what sense, each provides evidence of Joan's unusual powers:
   a) Joan's interview with de Baudricourt
   b) the death of Foul Mouthed Frank
   c) Joan's recognition of the Dauphin.
7. Analyse the different reasons for which the Chaplain, Cauchon and Warwick oppose Joan. Have you any sympathy with these reasons?
8. 'The theme of the freedom of the individual versus social order is central to *Saint Joan*; but it remains a complex and problematic issue, which the play does not resolve.' Discuss.
9. Whose side does Shaw take, Joan's or her judges'?

Part 5

Suggestions for further reading

The text

SHAW, GEORGE BERNARD: *Saint Joan: a Chronicle Play in Six Scenes and an Epilogue*, Constable, London, 1924. The first English edition of the play.

Saint Joan and *The Apple Cart*, Constable, London, 1949. The Standard Edition, now replaced by the Bodley Head definitive edition.

The Bodley Head Bernard Shaw: Collected Plays with their Prefaces, edited by Dan H. Laurence, Max Reinhardt, The Bodley Head, London, 1973, volume 6. This edition includes useful supplementary material, such as Shaw's programme note for the first English production, and the text of his radio talk of 1931, first printed in *The Listener*.

Saint Joan, Penguin Books, Harmondsworth, 1946, with many subsequent reprints. The text conforms to the definitive Bodley Head edition.

Saint Joan, with Introduction and notes by A. C. Ward, Longmans, London, 1957. This contains a good introduction and notes.

Other works by Shaw

SHAW, GEORGE BERNARD: *Complete Prefaces*, Paul Hamlyn, London, 1965.

Complete Plays, Paul Hamlyn, London, 1965.

Plays relevant to *Saint Joan*, such as *Caesar and Cleopatra, The Man of Destiny, Man and Superman, Major Barbara* and *Back to Methuselah* may be found in *The Bodley Head Bernard Shaw: Collected Plays with their Prefaces*, vols. 1–7, or in Penguin paperbacks. *Caesar and Cleopatra* appears in the volume *Three Plays for Puritans*, Penguin, 1946, and *The Man of Destiny* in *Plays Pleasant*, Penguin, 1946.

SHAW, GEORGE BERNARD: *The Quintessence of Ibsenism*, is reprinted in *Shaw and Ibsen: Bernard Shaw's The Quintessence of Ibsenism and*

Related Writings, edited with an introductory essay by J. L. Wisenthal, University of Toronto Press, Toronto, Buffalo, London, 1979.

Works on Shaw

BENTLEY, ERIC: *Bernard Shaw*, second British edition, Methuen, London, 1967. An intelligent study of Shaw's thought, and a useful critical survey of the plays.

CROMPTON, LOUIS: *Shaw the Dramatist: A Study of the Intellectual Background of the Major Plays*, University of Nebraska Press, Nebraska, 1969; Allen and Unwin, London, 1971. The chapter on *Saint Joan* deals with literary antecedents, and discusses the play in relation to Hegelian and Aristotelian theories of tragedy.

DUKORE, BERNARD F.: *The Collected Screenplays of Bernard Shaw*, edited with an Introduction, George Prior, New York, 1980.

GIBBS, A. M.: *Shaw*, Writers and Critics series, Oliver and Boyd, Edinburgh, 1965. An excellent short study.

HENDERSON, ARCHIBALD: *Bernard Shaw: Playboy and Prophet*, Appleton, New York and London, 1932. A detailed biography.
Bernard Shaw: Man of the Century, Appleton, New York, 1956. An updated version of his book of 1932.

KAUFMANN, R. J. (ED.): *G. B. Shaw: A Collection of Critical Essays*, Prentice Hall, Englewood Cliffs, New Jersey, 1965. A useful collection of essays, which includes an article by Louis Martz, 'The Saint as Tragic Hero: *Saint Joan* and *Murder in the Cathedral*'.

MEISEL, MARTIN: *Shaw and the Nineteenth-Century Theatre*, Princeton University Press, London, 1963. A useful and stimulating account of Shaw's indebtedness to Victorian dramatic conventions, including those of historical drama.

MORGAN, MARGERY M.: *The Shavian Playground: An Exploration of the Art of George Bernard Shaw*, Methuen, London, 1972. A penetrating analysis of the plays, particularly strong on mythic and ritualistic elements. Compares *Saint Joan* to pantomime and Passion Play.

PEARSON, HESKETH: *Bernard Shaw: His Life and Personality*, St James's Library, Collins, London, 1950; third edition, Methuen, London, 1961.

VALENCY, MAURICE: *The Cart and the Trumpet*, Oxford University Press, New York, 1973.

WARD, A. C.: *Bernard Shaw*, Longman, London, 1951. A good introduction to Shaw.

The author of these notes

ANNE WRIGHT was educated at the University of London, King's College, and her doctoral thesis was a study of George Bernard Shaw's *Heartbreak House*. She has taught at the universities of London and Lancaster, and at the Hatfield Polytechnic, where she is now Head of English Literature. In 1979 she received a British Academy Award which enabled her to research the collection of manuscripts and early texts of Shaw and D. H. Lawrence held at the University of Texas Humanities Research Center. Her publications include *Heartbreak House: A Facsimile of the Revised Typescript*, co-edited with Stanley Weintraub in the series *Bernard Shaw Early Texts: Play Manuscripts in Facsimile* (1981), and *Literature of Crisis 1910–1922*: Howards End, Heartbreak House, Women in Love and The Waste Land (1983). She has also written critical biographies of Harley Granville Barker and Tom Stoppard.